# CAMBRIDGE LIBRARY COLLECTION

*Books of enduring scholarly value*

## British and Irish History, Nineteenth Century

This series comprises contemporary or near-contemporary accounts of the political, economic and social history of the British Isles during the nineteenth century. It includes material on international diplomacy and trade, labour relations and the women's movement, developments in education and social welfare, religious emancipation, the justice system, and special events including the Great Exhibition of 1851.

## What Is to be Done for Ireland?

The Irish scientist John Ball (1818–89), active in the study of natural history and glaciology, held fellowships of both the Royal Society and the Linnean Society. When the Irish Potato Famine took hold, Ball returned from European travel and study intent on helping his countrymen. In 1846 he became an assistant poor law commissioner, and witnessed the deepening crisis at first hand. The first edition of this pamphlet was published in 1847. Reissued here is the second edition of 1849, the year when Ball assumed the more senior office of second poor law commissioner. He uses the pamphlet to argue passionately for the urgent revision of government legislation relating to poor relief, the public works programme, land improvement, labour and taxation, which he felt had exacerbated matters. He also believed the famine had been forgotten by the English and calls for them to show more sympathy towards the Irish.

Cambridge University Press has long been a pioneer in the reissuing of out-of-print titles from its own backlist, producing digital reprints of books that are still sought after by scholars and students but could not be reprinted economically using traditional technology. The Cambridge Library Collection extends this activity to a wider range of books which are still of importance to researchers and professionals, either for the source material they contain, or as landmarks in the history of their academic discipline.

Drawing from the world-renowned collections in the Cambridge University Library and other partner libraries, and guided by the advice of experts in each subject area, Cambridge University Press is using state-of-the-art scanning machines in its own Printing House to capture the content of each book selected for inclusion. The files are processed to give a consistently clear, crisp image, and the books finished to the high quality standard for which the Press is recognised around the world. The latest print-on-demand technology ensures that the books will remain available indefinitely, and that orders for single or multiple copies can quickly be supplied.

The Cambridge Library Collection brings back to life books of enduring scholarly value (including out-of-copyright works originally issued by other publishers) across a wide range of disciplines in the humanities and social sciences and in science and technology.

# What Is to be Done for Ireland?

JOHN BALL

CAMBRIDGE
UNIVERSITY PRESS

# CAMBRIDGE
## UNIVERSITY PRESS

University Printing House, Cambridge, CB2 8BS, United Kingdom

Cambridge University Press is part of the University of Cambridge.

It furthers the University's mission by disseminating knowledge in the pursuit of
education, learning and research at the highest international levels of excellence.

www.cambridge.org
Information on this title: www.cambridge.org/9781108077613

© in this compilation Cambridge University Press 2015

This edition first published 1849
This digitally printed version 2015

ISBN 978-1-108-07761-3 Paperback

# WHAT IS TO BE DONE

FOR

# IRELAND?

BY

## JOHN BALL, Esq., M.R.I.A.

LATE

ASSISTANT POOR LAW COMMISSIONER,

&c.     &c.     &c.

---

## SECOND EDITION.

---

London:

JAMES RIDGWAY, 169, PICCADILLY.

MDCCCXLIX.

# WHAT IS TO BE DONE

FOR

# IRELAND?

————◆————

THE present condition of Ireland—the nature
of the changes which are occurring beside us
and before our very eyes—the means of averting
the utter ruin which is impending over entire
provinces, and of protecting and maturing such
germs of improvement as appear to retain
vitality in the midst of the general confusion,—
these are topics of such engrossing importance,
and, at the same time, of such portentous difficulty, that no man who is interested in the
fortunes of the British Empire can well avoid to
consider them, while very few can with any
confidence pretend to offer a solution for the
perilous problems which they suggest.

It will lessen the appearance of presumption
on the part of a writer unknown to political
controversy to state, that in the following pages

I shall scrupulously avoid all personal, party, and sectarian questions. My object is simply to lay before the intelligent and well-disposed in either country a plain statement of authentic facts, having reference to the economical and social difficulties of the present crisis; not merely to awaken their attention, for this I believe has already been sufficiently accomplished, but further to assist them in arriving at practical conclusions by giving the results of anxious and painful inquiry and consideration— results based upon personal experience, assisted by frequent discussion with many of those most distinguished by knowledge, ability, and zeal for the public welfare.

I shall not be expected to enter into details, descriptive or historical, for the purpose of making known the condition of this country, or the causes which had produced that condition, at the period when, owing to the failure of the potato crop in the years 1845 and 1846, the social revolution commenced whose progress we still contemplate and whose results must for a long period decide our destinies. The entire world has resounded with our complaints; in every civilised tongue our miseries, our dissensions, our wrongs, and our vices, have been discussed and recorded. Those who do not already know whatever may be learned by mere reading are little likely to be informed by any attempt of mine. The sequel of our history up to the spring of the present year is scarcely less well known, and may be summed up in a few pages.

The partial failure of the potato crop, in the spring of 1846, was met by the timely introduction of a moderate supply of Indian corn meal*. The able-bodied poor who had lost their only means of subsistence were employed upon public works. The entire cost of relief during this season was £.733,372, of which sum £.368,000 is repayable to the Treasury from the county rates. The local subscriptions officially reported to the Government amounted to £.98,000; but allowance must be made for other private expenditure for relief purposes, and a large addition for the value of grain consumed in Ireland, which would, under ordinary circumstances, have been exported, and there will not be much error in estimating the direct cost of the first failure of the potato crop at about a million sterling.

The history of the succeeding year is even better known. In a few weeks the staple food of a population of five millions was all but utterly destroyed. A famine, perhaps the most fearful in its extent of any recorded in history, followed with awful suddenness. To say that the measures adopted by the Government were

* The amount provided for the relief service was 98,810 quarters, of which 84,235 quarters were sold up to August 1846.

insufficient to prevent misery, disease, and actual starvation, is not a ground of just reproach, for the visitation was one which no amount of legislative or administrative skill could effectually relieve. The system of employment upon public works, which had been used with tolerable success during the preceding season, was adopted with some modifications of detail. Whether from a reluctance to credit the estimated extent of the failure, though derived from the most authentic sources, or from an erroneous calculation of the resources existing in the country, the inevitable consequences of this measure were not perceived. Introduced by the Government at the close of the session, the Bill passed without a word of warning or remonstrance from any of the Irish members of the House of Commons*. The obvious and direct objections to a system of public works, as a means of relief during a period of general famine, are—the increased cost, amounting to fully double that of direct relief in food; the impossibility of effectual superin-

* In the House of Lords, Lord Monteagle pointed out the dangerous consequences of the proposed measure, and before the Bill had passed a strong remonstrance was drawn up and forwarded to the Prime Minister, at a meeting at which were present, the Earl of Devon, Sir Richard Bourke, Mr. Spring Rice, Mr. Monsell, Sir Vere de Vere, Sir David Roche, and several others of the most influential proprietors of the county of Limerick; these partial efforts were, however, completely unheeded.

tendence where a large portion of the population become applicants for relief; the hardships and the demoralisation caused by assembling together all the applicants for relief, whether able-bodied, infirm, or diseased, and requiring them to go through the form of out-door work in the midst of an inclement season ; and, worst of all, the permanent injury to the habits of the labouring class, when, through the want of sufficient check and inspection, they become familiarised with a system of *sham-work*, and lose every incentive to earnest industry.

But in addition to these evils there was another, which has not yet been generally understood in England, and which can be fully appreciated only by those conversant with the peculiar condition of this country.

In spite of unfavourable circumstances, arising from political and social causes, a period of industrial improvement had commenced in Ireland. Amongst other indications, the formation and progress of the Irish Agricultural Society sufficiently proves that a considerable number of proprietors had become alive to the necessity for improvement in the art of the cultivation of land, which had continued in a wretchedly imperfect and semi-barbarous state*. Some amongst them,

* Once for all I should remark, that, from most general statements, such as that given above, I except the more fortunate districts of Ulster and Leinster, where favourable

prompted by feelings of duty or of enlightened self-interest, had also begun to exert themselves in earnest to improve the condition of the poorer classes, whether small farmers or labourers, upon their estates. Upon the whole, gradual and steady, though not rapid progress was apparent throughout nearly the whole of Ireland; every year was marked by an increased expenditure of capital in farming; and gradually the tenant farmers were beginning to lose the prejudices and the ignorance which have proved an effectual bar to all improvement on their part. It was necessary that a certain number of persons of superior capital and education should take the lead in a movement of this nature; their influence could only gradually be felt upon the general mass, and it was obvious that a long period must elapse before the farmers could be got to feel any real interest in the amelioration of the condition of the labouring class.

circumstances acting upon an industrious race have produced, and still maintain, a considerable degree of material prosperity. One of the difficulties that arise in speaking or writing about Ireland proceeds from the fact that scarcely any assertion can be made which is generally true. Not only the whole island, but almost every separate county, exhibits within it the most strange contrasts in respect to the condition of its inhabitants. Variations, as marked as those which distinguish Tuscany from the most impoverished districts in Poland, may be found within the space of a few miles.

In proportion as it has been natural to feel indignation at the manner in which a large proportion of the proprietors of this country have forgotten their duties, neglected opportunities, and sacrificed their own interests and those of their successors to careless indolence or self-indulgence, so it was but just to prize the conduct of those who have pursued an opposite course, and upon whose exertions the progress of civilisation must for a long period materially depend. Men of the class here described had for the most part supported the poor of their own neighbourhoods during the spring of 1846 by subscriptions, to which some additional grants were made by the Government; but in the autumn of the same year they found that the only adequate means provided for the relief of a population which had suddenly lost their chief and almost exclusive means of subsistence was by public works. The presentments for the purposes of this Act were made by the magistrates and cess-payers assembled at Sessions, for each respective barony, half-barony, county of a city, or county of a town, in which relief was required. A barony in Ireland includes, upon an average, an area of about 65,000 acres, and a population of about 25,000. The rate-payers of each of these large districts were held jointly responsible for the support of famishing multitudes, and at a time when proprietors received but a small per centage upon their rents, and when all but the large farmers were in a state bordering on destitution, they were required to contract loans often exceeding in amount the entire annuul value of the district, repayment of which loans as they were informed would be rigidly enforced.

Although no one can without hesitation differ from so high an authority as Sir Charles Trevelyan, I confess that I cannot concur in his opinion that the measure here described was calculated to induce, or even to permit, of an increased expenditure of capital upon the cultivation and improvement of land*. Such an idea must have rested upon one of two suppositions, each of which appears to me equally untenable. Either it was supposed that a general co-operation of individuals and classes, resident and non-resident, solvent and insolvent, proprietors, middle-

* " The plan of the Labour Rate Act (9 & 10 Vict., c. 107) was based on the supposition that the great majority of the landlords and farmers would make those exertions, and submit to those sacrifices, which the magnitude of the crisis demanded, leaving only a manageable proportion of the population to be supported by the Board of Works; and the Act would probably have answered its object, if a larger instead of a smaller number of persons than usual had been employed in the cultivation and improvement of the land, and the Relief Committees had only put those who were really destitute upon the lists." (*Irish Crisis, p.* 31.) It will be recollected that the same opinion was expressed in a letter written by Lord John Russell, and published in the newspapers during the winter of 1846.

men, and farmers, could suddenly be brought
about by the magic of an Act of Parliament, or
else, that those who had hitherto taken a lead in
improvements were men of such abundant capital
that, in spite of present losses and prospective
taxation, they could afford to invest any required
amount of money in improvements with a view
to a future remunerative return.

With respect to general co-operation, I ven-
ture to doubt whether in districts of such extent
it could have been attained in any country in
Europe, save in peculiar and exceptional cases;
and I feel assured that no one practically conversant with this country for one moment admitted the possibility of realising a prospect so
illusory. Nor was the second supposition better
founded. It had long been a matter of notoriety
that the great majority of Irish properties were
heavily burdened with debt and with charges
created by family settlements, and that even
amongst the less incumbered the instances of
proprietors possessing large money capital were
but rare exceptions.

It is therefore no subject for surprise that the
Labour Rate Act to a great extent paralysed the
exertions of improving landlords. Those who
lamented the effects of the law could not take
upon themselves the responsibility of declining
its provisions. They could not encounter the
risk of leaving a large population of destitute

poor to precarious support to be obtained from private employment, and, with diminished means, they could not reserve their funds to meet heavy taxation, and at the same time expend those funds in carrying on measures of improvement upon their properties.

Though these views had not been stated in Parliament, they were not unfelt amongst practical men in Ireland. Very soon after the passing of the Act, Mr. Monsell (now M. P. for the county of Limerick) addressed a letter * to Mr. Labouchere, then Chief Secretary for Ireland, advocating a plan by which parties liable for a certain amount of rates should be enabled to cause that amount to be expended in reclamation or improvement of land under the superintendence of the Board of Works. This plan was warmly supported by many intelligent persons in this country, and was understood to have met the approval of the then Lord-Lieutenant, the late Earl of Besborough. It is not now desirable to discuss the merits of such a proposition, but I think it but just to remind my readers that the evils of the public works system were very early perceived and denounced, and that it is therefore incorrect to maintain that no alternative existed, other than that costly and ruinous experiment. In point of fact the movement did produce some effect. On the 5th of

* See extracts from this letter in the Appendix, p. 87.

October Mr. Labouchere published a letter,
addressed to the Board of Works, by which the
Commissioners were authorised to advance funds
upon presentments for drainage of lands, and
for subsoiling in connection with drainage, upon
condition that the proprietors of the land so
improved should consent that their estates should
be chargeable with the sums so advanced. This
measure obviated to a great extent the objections
which had made the general Acts for improvement and drainage unavailing to proprietors at
such a crisis : the cumbrous preliminary proceedings required by those Acts would have left
the people to starve before employment could
have been given by advances, to be obtained
according to their provisions; while the proceedings sanctioned by Mr. Labouchere's letter
required no other delay than that necessary
for obtaining competent superintendence. But
there remained the main objection, that in the
great majority of instances a proprietor who
borrowed money for improvements would diminish, but to a very slight extent, the pressure
of taxation to which he was already liable, and
the circumstances of but few, even of those who
most desired to avail themselves of the facilities
offered, allowed them to incur such an accumulated load of taxation. These difficulties
were stated in a memorial addressed to the
Lord-Lieutenant by the Reproductive Employ-

ment Committee\*. In spite of this objection, however, and although the presentments for public works had in most districts been already passed, and those works had actually been commenced, there was no indisposition to take advantage of the provisions of Labouchere's letter†. Upon the application of separate proprietors, presentments for £.380,607 was passed at sessions, and if, owing to a subsequent change in the law, not more than £.180,000 was actually expended, the fact is in no manner attributable to those proprietors who did everything on their part which the law permitted.

In the foregoing analysis of the system of public works introduced at the commencement of the famine of 1846, nothing can be farther from my mind than to impute blame to the framers of that measure; but, considering the misconceptions which still exist on this subject, I think it important that its tendency and results should be fully understood. It is very questionable whether by any modification, either of the objects or the machinery of such a system, it could have been made effectual for the relief of so

* See Appendix, p. 95.

† The proceedings sanctioned by that letter, were subsequently rendered valid by an Act passed at the commencement of the following session, by which also the Labour Rate Act was further amended by giving power to the Commissioners of Public Works to reduce the area of taxation from baronies to electoral divisions.

fearful a mass of destitution; but I have no
hesitation in expressing my belief that if the
pressure had been so distributed as not utterly
to restrain the application of enterprise and
capital to the cultivation and improvement of
land, the resources of this country would at this
time have been very considerably increased.

The public works, though administered with
untiring energy by men of the highest ability*,
became at length utterly unmanageable. To
create within a few months the staff and
machinery for the effectual direction and control
of an army numbering three-quarters of a million, was a task that exceeded the powers of any
public department; the system was abandoned,
but not before an expenditure had been incurred
of little less than five millions sterling. The
system of direct relief in food, which was substituted, fully established its intended object. At
the comparatively moderate cost of £.1,557,212,
an average number of a million and a half of the
population, including children, were effectually
fed for a period of nearly five months.

No sufficient data exist for estimating the
amount of capital lost to Ireland by the failure
of the potato and oat crops in the year 1846.

* The direction of the proceedings under the Public
Works Act, was confided almost exclusively to two of the
Commissioners of Public Works, Mr. Griffith and Captain
Larcom.

The loss arising from the deprivation of the staple food of a country is not the ordinary money-cost of that food, but the value of the new food which is substituted for it. The cost of the maize imported into Ireland during the season is estimated at about nine millions sterling, and about one million may be allowed for other descriptions of grain—rice, rye, buck wheat, &c. To this should be added the loss from diminished exports of wheat and oats to England, owing either to the loss on a deficient oat-crop, or to the necessity of using these articles as food in the place of potatoes. Another formidable source of loss, was the necessity of sacrificing live stock, especially pigs and poultry, which could no longer be fed with profit upon the expensive food which alone was procurable. Nothing gave so vivid an impression of the ruinous effects of the famine, even in the more prosperous districts, as the utter disappearance of pigs and poultry, the characteristic accompaniments of an Irish landscape. The loss in 1846 was nearly limited to the difference between the price of fattened animals in ordinary times and their reduced value when sold young or in bad condition during a glut of the market; but in the following season these important sources of income to the small farmers of Ireland had almost disappeared. From the Parliamentary returns of live stock, taken in the year 1847, it appears that the number of pigs upon farms less than fifteen statute acres had been reduced to one-eighth of the number found on the same farms in 1841, and the entire number in Ireland was considerably less than one-half of that given in the returns of the former period. So, also, the small farmers had lost nearly three-fourths of their stock of poultry, and for the country at large it had been diminished by one-third. These results are much more striking when we examine into the details and observe the losses which have fallen upon separate districts. Thus, in the province of Connaught, upon 112,132 holdings of less than fifteen statute acres there were, in 1847, but 15,768 pigs, and the whole number in the province was less than one-fourth of that given in the census of 1841.

The cost of imported food was defrayed in part from the funds granted from the Imperial Exchequer, consisting of the following principal items :—

| | £. |
|---|---|
| Half the expenditure under the Labour Rate Act . . . | 2,425,000 |
| Grants under the Temporary Relief Act . . . . . . | 714,529 |
| Grants in aid of Relief Committees . . . . . . . | 189,914 |
| Total . . | £.3,329,443 |

The entire of this sum was not expended upon

the purchase of food, but we may assume that about £.3,000,000 were so applied, and we should allow about £.500,000 for the amount of voluntary subscriptions transmitted to Ireland from England and from foreign countries*. The remaining £.6,500,000 were derived from the capital existing in Ireland, or from the loans authorised by Parliament, which are now in course of repayment. Adding £.8,500,000 for the loss arising from diminished exports, we may estimate at fifteen millions the actual loss to Ireland from the failure of the crops in 1846, without including the increase of poor-law taxation.

In 1847 the harvest was generally good, and the failure of potatoes was but slight and partial; but the income of the country was nevertheless considerably reduced, more especially in the western districts. In the first place there was a considerable outlay for seed potatoes imported into Ireland, and for seed of other crops intended to replace them; a certain proportion of arable land occupied by small farmers remained untilled owing to the want of seed; and the crops substituted for potatoes were less productive: there remained, therefore, a smaller surplus available for exportation; and as has already been explained the exportation of swine and cured pork, poultry, and eggs, was very materially diminished.

* The amount of contributions in food is of course not taken into this account.

But another important result of the loss of the potato crop remains to be considered. The cessation of the con-acre system, the impossibility of supporting a family upon farms of the smallest class with any other description of food, and the great diminution of demand for labour in farming, owing to the diminution of capital in the hands of the employers, and to the panic which seized the farmers throughout the greater part of Ireland—these causes, added to the increased disposition of the peasantry to rely upon public support, led to a fearful increase both of real destitution and of fictitious claims for relief. The Poor Law Extension Act had made the rateable property of Ireland liable, without limit, for the support of this entire mass of destitution, and it was the duty of the Poor Law Commissioners to enforce its provisions by all the means placed at their disposal by the Legislature. The result has been that while the poor-rates collected during the year ending 29th September, 1845, amounted to about £.300,000, the collection for the year ending 29th September, 1848, had reached £.1,700,000, showing an increase of £.1,400,000 expended from the resources of Ireland without any return whatsoever*.

* It must also be recollected that the Poor Law Extension Act was not in full operation during the early part of the period here mentioned.

Putting together these data we may estimate the loss of capital during the season of 1847–48* at about five millions sterling. We can now appreciate the position of Ireland in the autumn of 1848. During the three preceding years she had lost nearly seventeen millions and a half of capital (money or money's worth), and she had incurred a debt of £.3,754,739, which, even taking into account the remission of local taxation for the constabulary force, entails an increase of £.124,000 in the annual taxation for ten years, and the repayment within one or two years of nearly a million sterling. After all this there remained the increase of taxation for poor relief, which, in the present state of the population, cannot, even under favourable circumstances, be taken at less than £.1,500,000 per annum. I have not taken into account the expenditure under the Land Improvement Act, and the previous Drainage Acts. While, on the one hand, there is reason to hope that the outlay under those Acts will be reproductive, and that the resources of the country, after repayment of the money advanced, will be materially increased, and thereby be enabled to afford subsistence to an additional portion of the population; it should not be forgotten that the extraordinary expendi-

---

* It is obviously more convenient, for the purposes of this inquiry, to take the interval between the harvest of each successive year.

ture thus maintained, has supported a greater number of labourers than will ultimately find profitable employment upon the lands improved, and therefore if no adequate means be found for ensuring an increased demand for the labour now absorbed in the execution of works of drainage and improvement, an additional mass of unemployed labour will be thrown upon the poor-rates for support, and from this source alone we may calculate upon an annual addition of from £.200,000 to £.300,000 to the local taxation of Ireland. Thus, even though it be quite true that the present expenditure will ultimately be profitable to all parties, yet there is no doubt that the repayment of these advances, amounting on the whole to about £.200,000 a-year for eleven years, will, so long as the country remains in its present condition, be an additional source of embarrassment to proprietors in the poorer parts of Ireland.

Such was our condition; men who were in a position to appreciate the dangers and difficulties, the resources and the hopeful symptoms, were disposed to believe that throughout a great part of Ireland the elements of progress might overcome the present pressure, and that a period of toil and privation would be followed by an era of industrial energy and consequent prosperity. With respect, however, to the unfortunate districts of the west of Ireland, it was hoped, rather than expected, that the circumstances of the times, aided by the operation of the Encumbered Estates Act, passed during the last Session of Parliament, would lead to so large an investment of capital in the purchase and cultivation of land as might secure future means of subsistence for the famishing population. No one, that I know of, pretended to explain how that population was to be supported until the advent of better times.

Our destinies thus appeared to hang trembling in the balance when, during the last autumn, we received the certain intelligence of a fourth failure of the potato crop, which had promised an abundant harvest from an extent of land larger than it had ever before occupied, and of a loss upon the wheat crop of one-half the bulk, and two-thirds of the weight of grain throughout the southern half of the island. I believe that it is understating the case to allow seven millions sterling for the loss of the potato crop, and three millions for that of the wheat crop, during the present season. Thus it is an undeniable fact, that at this critical period of our fortunes we have had to sustain a further infliction in the shape of the destruction of £.10,000,000 of the annual income, out of which the subsistence of our population and the fund for the employment of labour have to be provided.

We may now make a summary estimate of

our losses during the four years from 1845 to
1848:—

|  |  |  | £. |
|---|---|---|---:|
| Direct cost to Ireland of the |  |  |  |
| failure of | 1845 | | 700,000 |
| „ | „ | 1846 | 11,500,000 |
| „ | „ | 1847 | 5,000,000 |
| „ | „ | 1848 | 11,400,000 |

Total of direct cost - - - - £.28,600,000

| Debt repayable on account of | | £. |
|---|---|---:|
| the failure of | 1845 | 368,000 |
| „ | „ 1846* | 3,754,739 |

Total debt repayable to the
Exchequer - - - - £.4,122,739

But a very imperfect idea can be formed of the
real amount of the pressure, if it is not recollected that this total loss of nearly thirty-three
millions is not uniformly distributed over the
entire island, but that on the contrary the far
greater portion of the burden has fallen upon
the south and west of Ireland. Here it was that
the cultivation of the potato was most extensively
spread, and that population compared with the

* The remission of one-half the cost of the constabulary
force amounting to £.192,000 per annum is not taken into
this account.

means of subsistence was most excessive; thus the direct loss and the pressure of increased taxation have alike fallen upon the very districts which were least able to sustain them.

It was necessary that I should at the outset of these remarks endeavour to bring distinctly before the minds of my readers the realities of our situation, too much forgotten, as it appears to me, by writers and speakers upon both sides of the Channel. No nation that I know of has ever had to support such heavy inflictions, through agencies beyond human control, within so short a period. Suffering and privation have become to a great extent inevitable; we in Ireland who are weighed down by the pressure, must recollect that although it may be within the power of Government to do a little to assist us in our endeavours to help ourselves, yet the burden has been placed upon our shoulders, and every man must be prepared to feel his share of the weight.

On the other hand it is scarcely less desirable that our case should be fairly understood and considered in England. It has not been owing, at least directly, to want of industry or skill, or to any of the other defects which are laid to our charge, that these grievous and repeated calamities have borne us to the earth. It may be in a great degree by our own fault that we have been poor, ill-fed, and ill-clothed; but for the causes which reduced poverty to general destitution, and bad food to starvation, we are not responsible. To our wealthy neighbours our losses may appear supportable, but if they will compare them with our means, or imagine to themselves a proportional loss out of their so much vaster resources, they will admit that our case is one that rather merits sympathy than contempt and opprobrium.

As one who bore an humble part in the work of relieving the unequalled mass of misery which in 1846 and 1847 called forth in so noble a manner the best feelings of Englishmen, I am entitled to bear testimony to the greatness of the efforts then made by individuals and by Government; and to the earnestness, zeal, and self-devotion of those whose duties or whose voluntary charity led them to labour in the cause; but it can never be sufficiently regretted that at the very period when such national exertions and sacrifices were freely and properly made, the publications which were believed to represent most truly the feelings of the English people, should have overflowed with an unceasing torrent of indiscriminate ridicule, abuse, and contempt for the objects of their benevolence. No right-minded man could complain of the exposure of individual cases of misconduct; it is even a misfortune to this country that we want organs of public opinion sufficiently honest and fearless to maintain a high standard of public morality by bringing such offenders to the bar of public opinion; but it was lamentable that at a time when the poorer classes were exhibiting to the world unexampled patience under intense suffering, when the great majority of the resident gentry and clergy of all persuasions were freely devoting their means and their unceasing labour to the performance of their duties, occasional instances of turbulence or impatience, of apathy, unreasonable complaint, or dishonesty, should have become pretexts for denunciations in which the names of Ireland and Irishmen were constantly identified with the objects of just or unjust vituperation. How often have I seen the same post which awakened gratitude by the intelligence of succour from British munificence carry with it printed provocations to indignation against British superciliousness and injustice. When the history of the time is fairly written the same stern condemnation which awaits those who, forgetful of recent benefits, could seek to excite in Ireland a blind hostility against England, will not less surely be awarded to those who contributed to the same object by embittering the feelings of Englishmen towards Ireland, and making the very benefits conferred by them wear the garb of injuries*.

Whether the general interests of the empire,

* The reader cannot have failed to peruse Mr. Aubrey de Vere's eloquent volume "English Misrule and Irish Misdeeds," in which this subject is admirably treated.

its financial condition, or the real necessities of Ireland, may make it the duty of Government to do much or little, or nothing for the direct relief of our population, it will still be true that our position is one difficult and painful enough to deserve the earnest sympathies of all who are not wrapped up in selfish indifference to the fate of their fellow-men.

It is fortunate that at the outset I can expect agreement amongst all classes of my readers. It is admitted, with one consent, that the pressing and universal evil under which we labour is poverty ; that the produce of the land is insufficient to support the people in comfort ; and all agree that the chief hope of improvement in our condition depends upon the increased application of labour and capital to agriculture ; that this increase of production, admitted to be the first requisite for any improvement in our condition, can be effected in but two ways :—by the full employment of those resources which we already possess, and by the introduction of new enterprise and capital from without. It is to be feared that the expectations of those who lead public opinion in England are too exclusively directed towards the latter alternative, and one of the objects which I propose to myself in these pages is to combat this tendency, which threatens to exercise a most disastrous influence over the destinies of this country.

At this point I desire distinctly to assert my belief, that both requisites for progress are alike indispensable, and that any course of legislation which tends to absorb the capital, or to discourage the industrial enterprise now existing in this country, will at the same time oppose an insurmountable bar to the so much desired influx of those elements. It is, I think, an error to present the case of the enterprising and industrious Irishman as an appeal *ad misercordiam,* or even as a claim founded merely upon abstract justice. True it is, that those men who have, against every variety of adverse circumstances, by industry, by patience and perseverance, developed the resources of impoverished districts, and commenced the great work of improvement in the habits and condition of their poorer fellow-countrymen, have the strongest claim that can be preferred to the sympathies and the justice of the Legislature ; still I maintain that the argument on their behalf rests upon the plainest grounds of economic policy, and that the interests of the entire empire are concerned in the fate of these men, who are now regarded with so much indifference.

The present race of improving proprietors and farmers possess the essential qualities which are required from men in their position, energy, enterprise, and skill ; and, in addition, they have that in which new comers will generally be deficient, a knowledge of the manners and disposition of the labouring class, and some share of their confidence. It may not be very difficult to destroy, or materially to diminish the numbers, already too limited, of this class, but to substitute others in their place would, under any circumstances, be a tedious operation; it may become impossible, if a system of legislation should prevail under which the qualities, which in a healthy state of society can command success, are here condemned to failure and ruin.

I propose, then, briefly to consider the means for providing due security for the investment of capital in agriculture by proprietors and tenant farmers; and for removing landed property from the hands of fictitious owners, and placing it in those of men able to exercise the rights and perform the duties attached to its possession. It will, therefore, be necessary for me to discuss the measures which either are in operation or have been proposed with reference to those objects, the Poor Law, the Landlord and Tenant Bill of last Session, the Encumbered Estates Act, and the laws affecting the transfer of real property. It will be advisable, moreover, to notice Emigration and Systematic Colonization, so far as these subjects immediately affect the condition of Ireland; and I shall offer a few remarks upon some of the other proposed measures of improvement which have been suggested.

The subject to which most of my observations

shall be directed, and which at this moment holds
the first place in importance amongst all classes in
this country, is, without doubt, the most important, and the most perplexing which the present state of society has forced upon the consideration of statesmen. Permanently to provide a
remedy for destitution, without at the same time
increasing the evil which it is the object of
legislation to cure, is the grand problem which
modern society has undertaken to resolve. I
believe that the more any man will study the
question, the more he will perceive and realise to
himself the difficulties which it presents. M.
Naville, the author of a valuable work upon this
subject*, in speaking of a discussion which took
place in Switzerland, between the supporters of
large and small areas for settlement and rating,
observes that the partisans of each opinion had a
great advantage in attacking the plan of their
adversaries, but showed extreme weakness when
reduced to defend their own views. This remark
appears to me equally applicable to all discussions
in which the principles of the Poor Law are
concerned, and to be inherent in the very nature
of the subject. If the faults of individuals, and
the vicious social relations, which are the causes
of pauperism, could be remedied by direct legislation, without entailing serious evil and incon-

* De la Charité Légale, de ses Effets, de ses Causes, &c.,
par F. M. L. Naville. Paris, 1836.

venience upon the community, there would be an exception to the general providential laws by which human relations are governed, and a failure of that stimulus by which society is urged onward in the path of progrets.

Permanent good can be effected only when it becomes possible to mitigate or destroy the causes of pauperism, but I am far from believing that on this accouut we should regard with indifference the course of direct legislation for the relief of the poor. It is the duty of the statesman to weigh the circumstances of his time and country, and to decide upon the course towards which the preponderating considerations shall incline.

Impressed with the extreme difficulty of the task, and admitting that, at the best, I can only hope for partial success, I hope to be excnsed for entering, at some little length, upon a topic which has engaged my most anxious and continued study and reflection.

In spite of the experience which has been gained at a heavy cost within the last few years both in this and in foreign countries, it seems as if but few persons had yet learned to moderate the conviction which is popularly entertained as to the power of a Government to alleviate poverty by *direct* interference for the relief of distress. A still less number probably have acquired definite ideas as to the conditions under which that power can justly or safely be exercised.

Although I have no desire to burden these pages by references to the principles of political economy, I think that an allusion to some of the plainest truths of that science may be borne with at a time when so many errors prevail even amongst the well-informed and sincere portion of the public.

It is an axiom which, were it not so frequently forgotten, one would think it unnecessary to assert, that the rights of labour are prior to every other right connected with property, whether the labourer till a plot of ground before unappropriated, or is employed for daily wages in the field, society, wherever anything deserving the name of Government exists, has always recognised his right to subsistence for himself and his family.

It is unnecessary here to consider how in civilised communities, where population has outstepped the limits within which each man is enabled to procure subsistence for himself and his family by the direct appropriation of natural products, the existence of a large portion of the labouring class is supported by that part of the accumulated results of previous labour which is called productive capital. This forms the fund for the employment of labour, and if this fund be diminished, or, more properly, if it do not annually increase in the same proportion as the labouring population, the result must be

either that less labourers will be employed or that
the same number of labourers must receive lower
wages. If in any country the rate of wages is
very nearly the lowest at which human life can
be supported, the effect of deducting a certain
sum from the wages-fund will be to take away
the means of subsistence from a proportional
number of labourers.

I need not here go into the detail of the reasons which induce me to admit that there is no
practical danger that a tax for the relief of the
helpless poor (including in that designation all
who are temporarily or permanently disabled
from labour by unprotected infancy, old age, in-
firmity, bodily or mental defect, or sickness),
administered under proper regulations, will in
any civilised community tend permanently to
diminish the fund for the employment of labour.
But it is important to remark that no *right to
relief* can be asserted on behalf of the above-
mentioned or any other class of the community,
unless this condition of leaving the wages-fund
inviolate be strictly complied with.

The same principle must guide and direct us
in considering the abstract justice or the political
expediency of a legal provision for the relief of
the destitute able-bodied poor. Even though
upon other grounds we should be persuaded that
such provision is justifiable and desirable, we

c

must be fully satisfied that it can be administered in such a manner as not to diminish the fund for the employment of labour. If the governing power in any country neglects or violates this condition, it is guilty at once of the grossest infraction of justice, and the most insane defiance of the plainest principles of common sense. For it can scarcely be necessary to point out that the diminution of the wages-fund in any one year tends, by increasing the mass of pauperism, to increase the burden for the following year; and if the cause which occasioned the original diminution continue in operation, it is evident that a continual increase of pauperism and a corresponding decrease of production must rapidly reduce such a community to a general level of misery.

I do not imagine that any reasonable mind can refuse assent to the principle here laid down, but I insist that it must not merely be admitted as true, but that it should be recognised as the governing law which must overrule every other consideration when we attempt to discuss the subject of legislation for the relief of the poor. The greatest errors in policy arise not so much from ignorance or blindness as to the facts and principles involved, as from a defective perception of their relative importance. Society and human legislation can advance only by a gradual progress;

we must be content to realise the good which we desire in that order in which Providence has made it possible to us. Impatient attempts to construct the upper portion of the fabric before we have secured the foundations do but impede real progress, and if rashly persisted in must involve extensive confusion and ruin.

As to the subject of a legal provision for the relief of the helpless poor, I do not think it necessary to discuss it at length. The course of legislation has of late years been altogether decisive in its favour, and it is supported by one argument, which appears to my mind altogether to outweigh all the objections of its opponents. The absence of a legal provision involves the permission of mendicancy, and the consequent growth of a class of outcasts from society, the children of beggars, who are left to increase from infancy to manhood without the hope or the opportunity of filling any useful place in society.

A large proportion of the class that subsists by begging will always be attracted towards the larger towns. I cannot conceive any consideration short of a belief in the utter impossibility of a remedy, which can induce any Christian community to tolerate the existence of the mass of suffering, disease, and crime which is inevitably inflicted upon this most helpless and pitiable class. Nor is it easier to understand how calculating men can fail to perceive the cost at which the growth of so expensive a disease is allowed to continue unchecked\*.

Regarding the question, however, merely in the economic point of view, there is no reason to admit that the cost of a legal system of relief to the helpless poor would press too heavily upon the resources of this country†. The estimate given in the annexed note amounts to a charge of about 6 per cent. upon the value of rateable pro-

---

\* I am far from being insensible to the serious imperfections of the education now given in workhouses, and I refer the reader to page 71, where this subject is resumed. Even in its present state the education of pauper children in Ireland is, probably, on the whole, superior to that given to the same class in England; where it is open to serious reproach the fault must be attributable to those who are locally responsible for the due administration of the law.

† It is not possible to ascertain with accuracy from the returns published by the Poor Law Commissioners the actual cost of relief given to the helpless poor in Ireland. Amongst the classes entitled to relief out of the workhouse under the first section of the Poor Law Extension Act are able-bodied widows having two or more legitimate children; these cannot properly be included under the denomination of *helpless poor*. From inquiries in various districts, I estimate the proportion of this class receiving relief at about one-fifth of the whole number relieved under the first section of the Act. I believe that if we allow £.500,000 for the annual cost of maintaining 100,000 of the helpless poor in workhouses at £.5 a head, and £.300,000 for 200,000 of the same class received out of the workhouse, at thirty shillings a head, we should fully meet the real requirements of this portion of the population.

perty. A tax of greater amount could probably be supported without any serious detriment to the industrial development of Ireland.

The serious difficulties of the subject commence when we approach the subject of relief to the able-bodied poor. The formidable fact with which we have to deal in Ireland is the absorption of a large portion of the productive capital of the country in the maintenance of the unemployed able-bodied population.

The facts already made public and the further evidence which is given in the Appendix, must be admitted to prove conclusively the fact that the wages-fund throughout a considerable part of Ireland has been diminished to a most serious extent. I shall give reasons for believing that the entire effect is not to be attributed to the operation of the Poor Law even in its present form; and I am very far from thinking that, by proper modifications of the law, it will be impossible to provide adequate relief for the able-bodied destitute poor without further impairing the resources of this country; but I have no hesitation in coming to the conclusion that if that object cannot speedily be attained, a continuance of the attempt to enforce the present law in the poorer districts will involve a greater amount of misery and desolation than the total discontinuance of relief to the able-bodied.

The one mode of administering relief to the

able-bodied poor, which experience has shown to be capable of restraining the unlimited growth of pauperism, is that of confining them in work-houses. Under no other system is it possible permanently to preserve the inducements to independent industry, and to avoid holding out to the labouring classes positive temptation to a servile dependence upon public support. The combined testimony of the most able, impartial, and philanthropic witnesses who have studied and observed the working of poor-laws in Europe and America, proves, without a doubt, that relief to the able-bodied, unaccompanied by restrictions which make their condition less desirable than that of the independent labourer, has had in every country where it has been introduced, the uniform tendency to lower the physical and moral condition of the poorer classes, and to check the development of industry throughout the entire community. The rapidity with which these evils are developed, depends upon the character and condition of the population of each country, but no doubt remains as to the ultimate result.

In Ireland, however, we have at the present time no need to appeal to the experience of other countries. With every allowance for the effects of the failure of crops, it is impossible to doubt the disastrous results of out-door relief to the able-bodied poor in these districts, where it has

become the duty of the Poor Law Commissioners
to issue orders for that purpose under the second
section of the Poor Law Extension Act. I
should multiply tenfold the Appendix to these
pages if I were to attempt to collect together the
published evidence on this subject. Parliamentary papers, reports from Inspectors of
Unions, daily newspapers, all concur in representing a most fearful deterioration in the habits
and disposition of our population, never accustomed to obtain by their imperfect industry more
than a bare subsistence, so soon as they are enabled to obtain food without any other restrictions
than such mockery of labour as it is alone possible to obtain by employment of paupers. There
is nothing in this which could surprise those who
know anything of the condition of the poorer
districts in Ireland; the same causes must have
produced the same consequences in any other
country in which the labouring class had become
habituated to nearly the lowest possible physical
condition.

There is no reason to believe that, in enacting
the recent changes in the Irish Poor Law, the
Government or the Legislature seriously contemplated that out-door relief to the able-bodied
should become an usual practice in any part of
Ireland. The Act expressly limits the period for
which the order authorising relief of this kind
shall remain in force to two months, and it is

but giving credit for an ordinary share of good sense to the authors of the Bill, to suppose that they had not utterly forgotten or disregarded the evidence and the advice of all the most competent persons belonging to either country, who have spoken or written upon the subject. Although, as is not unnatural, such charges are sometimes made by those who are suffering from the working of the present law, I will not believe that the Legislature has been so unmindful of its reponsibility to every portion of this vast empire, or so blind to the common interests which link together each member of the entire body, as carelessly to adopt an expedient which would, for a short time, postpone a present difficulty at the cost of the speedy disorganisation of society throughout one-third of Ireland.

I am persuaded that, even if some individuals were disposed, through impatience at the difficulty of the subject, or through an unprincipled desire to seek popularity in England at the expense of Ireland, to fling upon us a troublesome burden, without much heeding the conditions under which alone it could become supportable, the great majority of all parties in England were labouring under an honest misconception of the results of the proposed extension of the Poor Law. It was continually asserted and believed that the effect of the new law would be to induce the owners and occupiers of land to provide employment for the labouring class, and that efficient means had been provided for placing the land in the hands of *bonâ fide* proprietors, who would have adequate security for the remunerative investment of capital in improved agriculture.

That the present law, under the existing circumstances of more than half of Ireland, tends to restrict the expenditure of capital in agriculture on the part of the present proprietors and farmers, and to prevent the transfer of property to new holders possessed of skill and capital, are propsitions which have by this time been conclusively established. If, when the evidence of these facts shall be fully laid before Parliament, the Government should fail to attempt a remedy for a state of things so alarming, so fraught with irremediable ruin and confusion, they will go far to prove the truth of the worst charges which have been brought in this country against Imperial legislation.

With reference to the effect of the present Poor Law in checking agricultural improvement, I have endeavoured to take every means in my power for ascertaining the extent and nature of the evil. I have not contented myself with the statements which abound in every newspaper, but have examined for myself into the circumstances of many districts with which I am acquainted, and sought by observation and inquiry to arrive at an accurate knowledge of the truth*. The result has been to satisfy me that the mischief is not now universal throughout more than about one-third of the island, and that it extends partially through a remaining third: I believe, moreover, that the effect, especially amongst the farmers, is greater than the cause now justifies, and is in great measure due to a panic which, here as in other cases, tends very speedily to realise the worst evils which it apprehends.

With these reservations I must contend that the necessary result of the present law, is very frequently to place an absolute bar to the extension of productive industry. I am not now considering whether the law does or does not, should or should not *stimulate* the employers of labour —that is a separate question, to which I shall speedily allude. But when I find enterprising men, who had not waited for the pressure of the last few years to commence a course of improvement, who have actually succeeded in adding to the productiveness of the soil, and to the comfort of its inhabitants, forced to restrict or desist from their operations, not because these had ceased to be profitable to themselves and to those whom they employed, but because the means destined for the payment of wages had been taken from them for the support of the poor

* For evidence on this subject, see Appendix, p. 108.

upon neighbouring properties, I cannot doubt but that a mischief has been inflicted, not only upon the individual, but upon the entire community. That which I have here described has actually occurred in many instances, and I know that in very many others the means of employers are rapidly becoming exhausted, and they must soon arrive at the same result.

This portion of the existing evil, which I consider *necessary* in the present circumstances of this country, arises from the *actual amount* of taxation; the further and still more extensive portion, which is due to *panic*, depends upon the uncertainty of the amount of future taxation. None but the few landlords who possess a very large share of the property of an electoral division, and the still less number who are able, by co-operation with the other proprietors in the same division, to calculate the proportion between those who require support and the means for providing it, are able in the least degree to foresee or to make provision for the demands to which they may be subjected. So long as this country remains in the transition state in which the demand for labour is not a fixed ascertainable quantity, but one which depends upon the varying amount of capital and enterprise of those who now occupy the land, or of those who may speedily succeed them, this formidable degree of uncertainty must continue, and must still paralyse the exertions of all classes of employers. The apprehension arising from this cause is sufficiently potent with the proprietors; but with the tenant farmer, possessing less information and intelligence, and always disposed to exaggerate that which is unknown, the fear of increasing taxation has become a spectre which is daily driving hundreds of small capitalists to abandon their farms and depart with all that they can remove, to swell the wealth and increase the feelings of hostility to Great Britain in the United States of America. The man who has a hundred pounds available for the employment of labour cannot guess whether the rate which last month was £.10 may not become £.50 when the collector calls upon him in the ensuing spring. The neighbouring gentleman who now employs some hundreds of destitute labourers may be driven to discontinue that employment, as that other neighbour was last summer, and the rates must then be increased to an unknown and therefore thrice exaggerated amount. The farmer knows that he is ruined if unable to meet the collector's demand—his cattle and moveables must be sacrificed at a depreciated, often at a merely nominal, price. The result is that which we now behold—the farmers who remain turn off labourers and half cultivate their land; our ports are crowded with emigrants, chiefly the more industrious and provident of the tenant farmers of the south and west, who hasten to dispose of property and sacrifice everything in the desire to leave our shores*. It is useless to contend that this panic is in a great degree unfounded; that many of those who leave the country might, by good farming and industry, safely continue at home and realise comfort and independence; we must take our population such as we find them, and if we would not consummate the ruin of this country, we must put a stop to a state of things which is daily diminishing our remaining capital, and destroying every chance of improvement.

It is to the uncertain character of the poor-rate taxation that I attribute the chief part in the second evil result of the present law—the tendency to discourage the investment of new capital in the purchase and cultivation of land. So long as it is impossible for a man to form a reasonable estimate of the charges to which property may be subject, no one of common prudence will become a purchaser unless at an enormous depreciation, sufficient to cover with a wide margin the possible increase of taxation. This depreciation would be so serious through

* Such is the depreciation of produce, owing in part to emigration and in part to the actual distress of the farmers who remain, that good meat is now sold in some southern counties at two-pence per pound.

about half of Ireland, that the combined influence of creditors will generally prevent sales*. The prior incumbrances have no sufficient motive in urging on sales so long as they receive their interest, and subsequent creditors will generally prefer to submit to some loss and irregularity in the payment of interest, rather than risk the more serious loss of principal.

Thus we see that the policy which dictated the recent Encumbered Estates Act, principally with a view to the investment of new capital in land, is defeated by the present state of the law, and this fact is one which of itself should satisfy even those whose sympathies are altogether denied to the present proprietors of the necessity for change†.

Before I state the conditions which, according to my judgment, are indispensable for the suc-

---

* A small property in Fermoy Union, favourably circumstanced in having but a few considerable tenants, was sold, within the last few weeks, for twelve years' purchase.

† This is one of the points as to which persons little acquainted with Ireland are most exposed to error. One property may retain its full value, while the adjoining one is reduced by one-half or two-thirds, owing to local circumstances. Thus it is quite possible that a purchaser, with sufficient capital, might prudently give twenty years' purchase for a property in the worst parts of Mayo, and yet that no one could be found to give eight years' purchase for any other estate that will be offered for sale in that county for many years to come.

cessful working of the Poor Law in Ireland, I shall make a few observations upon a subject which has given rise to a difference of opinion amongst some of the most able men in this country.

It was frequently maintained in Parliament, by the supporters of the proposed Poor Law Extension Act, that one effect of making the employers of labour responsible for the support of the able-bodied poor would be to stimulate that class to devise means for the support of the labourer by independent employment at money wages. Subsequently it has been argued by some of those who desire the limitation of the area of rating to individual properties, that by this means only can a sufficient stimulus be given to the exertions of proprietors and farmers. To this it has been replied that it is a mistake to assume that it is the proper object of a Poor Law to give any stimulus to the holder of capital to expend that capital in employment. The true motive for expenditure is the prospect of a remunerative return; this will infallibly act in a free labour market, and any additional artificial stimulus will, if it act at all, tend to cause a less productive investment, and, therefore, to diminish the wealth of the community. Again, we are reminded that by a stimulus is meant some provision by which the proprietor who fails to provide employment, or, in other words, that the labourer should have a means of securing wages other than his own industry and good conduct.

It is impossible to deny that the last-mentioned arguments have great weight, and that in a healthy state of society they should be held conclusive. But the practical way to consider them is to examine whether the assumptions which they involve hold good in this country at the present time, when owing to the want of industrial enterprise of landlords and farmers they do not generally invest their capital in the way in which it would be most productive*, and owing to the defects of the law which impede the free transfer of land, and discourage purchasers, new capital does not flow in to supply the place of that which is either altogether wanting, or is lying unemployed in the hands of the present holders. There is no reason to fear that in practice any additional stimulus would create an unproductive outlay of capital in a country where such ample opportunities exist for its remunerative investment. On the other hand, I think that the workhouse test will always be a sufficient check to the wilful pauperism of labourers, and where that is absent the speedy pauperisation of the entire class is under one or the other system equally inevitable. I must

* See a letter from Mr. Monsell, M.P., published in the *Morning Chronicle* of the 23rd of December, 1848.

confess, however, that I am so sensible of the evils which a more stringent law of settlement (inseparable from property-rating) would produce, that I should not wish to see any change in the law which would involve the *permanent* chargeability of pauper labourers upon the separate estates where they are at present located, while I do not find that any less stringent measure than property-rating is adequate to meet the evils now pressing upon us. I shall speedily point out the mode in which I conceive that the difficulties attending the adoption of the principle may best be solved.

The objects which legislation in connection with the relief of destitution must accomplish are these:—It must not by excessive taxation withdraw from productive industry those funds which would otherwise be devoted to the maintenance of independent labourers, and therefore the actual or possible amount of assessment upon those proprietors who are engaged in the career of improvement should not be such as to prohibit or deter them from exertion; it should remove those obstacles by which the transfer of land to those who are able and willing to develop its resources are impeded, and it should not allow that operation to be delayed by the prospect of an overwhelming and unlimited amount of taxation; in districts where the existing resources are manifestly inadequate to the maintenance of

D

the inhabitants (proved by the impossibility of providing relief in workhouses for the able-bodied destitute poor) it should provide adequate means for the removal of a sufficient number of the population, instead of continuing a system by which the slender capital of such districts is rapidly absorbed, and the labouring class inured to habits of indolent dependence; lastly, it should restrain as far as possible that disposition to shift the burden of taxation which has acquired an infamous notoriety under the names of clearing or extermination. If in addition to these objects it should provide an additional stimulus to the employment of the labouring class in productive industry, the result would, in the present state of Ireland, be highly advantageous.

The various means by which it has been proposed to accomplish the conditions above stated, may be referred, with slight differences of detail, to three plans, each of which has been advocated by men of considerable practical ability: these are, the limitation of local taxation, the excess being supplied from national or imperial resources; the partial exemption from rating of persons paying a certain sum as wages; and, finally, the limitation of the area of rating to individual properties, with some provision for assistance to those properties which are manifestly unable to support the existing population.

Assuming that the Boundary Commissioners

appointed to investigate the propriety of altering
the limits of the present unions and electoral
divisions, will recommend a considerable subdi-
vision of the present area of chargeability, and a
closer adherence to the boundaries of estates, I
am of opinion that the limitation of the amount
of local taxation would mitigate to a great extent the evils of the present system. If when
the rate on any one electoral division amounted
to five shillings within the year, the excess were
charged to the union at large, and when the
separate union rate reached half-a-crown per
annum, public funds to be administered by public
officers were advanced to sustain or remove
the weight of local destitution, some confidence
would be restored to the improving landlord and
farmer, the panic which is driving men into
voluntary exile would be allayed, and the depreciation in the value of land, which at present restrains both purchaser and seller, would
find a definite and calculable limit. But I apprehend that this plan would but very imperfectly
remove the present discouragement to enterprise
in the improvement of land. But few would
feel that their position could be materially improved by their own exertions; the general
disposition of all classes when subjected to an
uniform pressure would be to accommodate themselves to it, and allow the amount of local pauperism to be partially relieved by public funds. It
may be, that in England the result would be

different; that the prospect of ultimate advantage would preserve the spirit of enterprise under such a weight of new taxation; but in a country where the desire for accumulation is much weaker, and where experience has not created confidence in the results of successful exertion, the addition of the immediate advantage of relief from taxation to the prospective benefits of agricultural improvements, is not more than the necessary inducement to that general and earnest effort to develop our latent resources, by which alone we can be raised from our present wretched and still sinking condition.

The plan of exempting from taxation for the relief of the able-bodied those who should find employment for the labourers upon a townland, or an entire property, has been advocated by several active and intelligent men. An outline of the details by which such a system should be worked has been drawn up and circulated by Mr. Crosbie*, one of the most active and im-

* See Appendix, p. 98. If any measure resembling this plan were adopted, it would be necessary that the person claiming exemption should have served a notice of his intention upon the Board of Guardians at the commencement of the half year, and it would be much better that the two rates proposed should be distinguished as rates for workhouses and out-door relief. This would limit the application of the system to those unions where the out-door relief is extensively given, but it would partially protect the employer against the misconduct of labourers, by allowing him without forfeiting his exemption to refer such labourers to the workhouse as an alternative for employment.

proving landlords in the south of Ireland. The
advantage possessed by this system over either of
the others here discussed is the security and
stimulus which it applies to the tenants as well
as to the landlords. The tenant occupying a
single townland, or a number of tenants co-
operating for the purpose, would feel themselves
free to apply the sum now paid as poor-rate to
the profitable employment of labourers.

I am far from undervaluing this advantage, and
if on other grounds it were allowable to accept
the plan, I should think this point a strong re-
commendation in its favour. But, in the first
place, owing to the extreme irregularity in the distribution of population, the effect of this plan
would be to withdraw from taxation all the less
populous and less pauperised townlands, leaving
those which contain villages and hamlets to be
burdened up to the extreme limit at which the
rate in aid should be applied. The second and
most formidable objection is the complete destruction of the freedom of the labour market, a result
which would no less certainly attend a proposed
modification of the same principle by which the
labouring population should be apportioned to
the several occupiers in the ratio of their valuation, or of the extent of arable land held by
them.

The terms and conditions of employment would
no longer depend upon the free action of the

employer and the labourer; they would be continually subjected to discussion and inquiry before
a tribunal, especially ill-fitted properly to decide
them. According to the bias of the Board of
Guardians, the employer would be in the power
of the labourer, or the labourer in that of the
employer.

The labourer would be *ad scriptus glebæ*, and
we should see a revival of evils which were
thought peculiar to a former state of society, and
which it was the especial object of the Poor Law
Amendment Act to eradicate in England. Under
the proposed plan the sympathies of the tenant
class would be enlisted on the side of the employer,
and being consequently sure of the support of
the guardians, complete control would be placed
in his hands. I confess that observation and
experience have made me very averse to any
system which would entrust the fate of the
labouring class so unreservedly to the charity and
forbearance of the landlords and farmers, as I
should equally object to see these at the mercy
of a body so ignorant and blind, even to their
own direct interest, as are the poorer class in this
country *.

* It is well known that many branches of native industry
have been partially or altogether driven from Ireland into
England and Scotland by the combinations of workmen who
have maintained rates of wages higher than those given to
skilful artisans on the other side of the Channel.

The third alternative which has been suggested is to make each separate property the area of chargeability and rating, leaving the electoral division as the area for representation. I think that it cannot be disputed by any one practically acquainted with this country, that this system would lead to a rapid extension of agricultural improvement, and though it would precipitate the already certain ruin of the owners of many encumbered and pauperised properties, it would afford the means of saving themselves to deserving men, who will otherwise be forced to share the fate of their neighbours. Assuming that a discretionary power were given to the Poor Law Commissioners to form towns into separate areas of rating, that a change in the law of settlement should make it less easy for the rural districts to throw their surplus pauperism upon the larger towns, and that an union rate should be applied in aid of those properties which would otherwise be utterly confiscated, there remain the objections of injustice to individuals, imperfect representation, and interference with the free employment of labour.

Injustice, that is, great inequality of taxation without corresponding deserts or demerits on the part of those taxed, is inevitable under any practicable system in the present state of this country. True it is, that I cannot in justice claim exemption from rating, because from some accident the prudence of a tenant, or the act of an ancestor, my property has few pauper inhabitants, less still can I do so if I have used my legal powers to drive them away to other estates or to the nearest town; but it is quite as little just that I should profit because the estates of two or three neighbouring proprietors are cleared, or that I should be ruined because they are overcrowded with unemployed labourers, whom they cannot or will not employ. We must be contented to deal with the unequal distribution of pauperism as a fact, and to mitigate its pressure upon those localities where it is insupportable.

With property-rating, the guardian elected for an electoral division would have no community of interest with the greater portion of those whom he would be supposed to represent. This is a serious objection, yet with competent relieving officers, and due watchfulness on the part of the owners or representatives of property, it would not be formidable nor comparable in importance to the other considerations involved in the question. It should be recollected that under the present system the guardian of a division of 15,000 or 20,000 acres must frequently be incompetent to determine the facts as to residence of an applicant for relief, whereas under property-rating the parties interested would always have access to the means of ascertaining the truth.

The interference in the relations between the employer and the labour, is without doubt the chief objection to property-rating. It would be probably less felt that under the system of exemption, where an employer undertakes to provide for a definite number of the able-bodied poor, but yet, though at first no material aggravation of the present state of things would be perceived, I apprehend that if permanently established it would place a bar to any real improvement in the condition of the labouring class. I agree to some extent with Mr. Monsell, who argues in his able letter to the *Morning Chronicle*, to which I have already referred, that the unhealthy relations between capital and labour which are anticipated by the opponents of property-rating already exist in this country, and must exist wherever the proportion of capital and labour is insufficient; but, admitting that this is true to a great extent, it scarcely furnishes an argument for a measure which would tend to perpetuate that portion of our present evils.

The reader will now ask whether I am prepared with any practical suggestions by which to reconcile the apparently incompatible objects which we desire to secure—adequate security for the investment of capital in agricultural improvement, and freedom in the relations between the employer and the labourer?

Aware of the disadvantages to which a writer

submits, who, instead of criticising the plans of others, ventures to produce propositions of his own, and fully persuaded of the impossibility of devising any course which shall be altogether unobjectionable, I proceed to give an outline of the measure which I would recommend.

Saving a general power to the Poor Law Commissioners to unite properties below a certain small area, and to constitute towns and even large villages, not belonging to the owner of adjacent lands, into separate divisions for the purposes of chargeability and rating, I would make the area for these purposes coincident with the boundaries of separate properties*. Whenever the rate leviable in any one year upon any such division exceeded five shillings in the pound sterling upon the existing valuation, the surplus should be carried to the account of the union at large. Whenever the rate leviable upon the union at large (which it must be remembered is in addition to that assessed upon each separate *rateable division*) exceeded half-a-crown in the pound, the guardians and the proprietors of any division should be empowered to apply to the Poor Law Commissioners, who should be authorised to apply funds to be advanced by the Treasury to assist such residents upon any

---

* The definition of a property being the estate of any one or more individuals qualified to apply as owners under the Land Improvement Act.

property in the union liable for more than five shillings in the pound as should be willing to emigrate.

One-half of such advances should be charged as a debt, repayable with interest in yearly instalments by the owner ; or, in the case of towns, by the ratepayers, of the rateable division relieved, the remaining moiety being a free grant. All advances for emigration purposes should be administered by an Inspector under the Poor Law Commissioners. The limits of electoral divisions for the purposes of representation should remain as at present, the report of the relieving officer as to the residence and chargeability of paupers being held conclusive, unless appealed against by a ratepayer, in which case it would be desirable that a Poor Law Inspector should have the power to hear and determine such appeals, awarding reasonable costs where the complainant or the relieving officer appeared guilty of haste, fraud, or negligence. The provisions of the present law as to chargeability of paupers should be altered in the following manner. Every person receiving relief should be chargeable to the rateable division on which he or she had resided or usually slept for thirty months within the four years preceding admission to relief, but not having so resided, to be charged to the union at large. Any person having been in receipt of relief in or out of the workhouse, again admitted to relief within twelve months from the time when such relief ceased should be chargeable to the same rateable division as before, but otherwise to be chargeable to the union at large. Any person appearing from the books of the union to have been, either continuously or at separate intervals, in receipt of relief for a period amounting altogether to four years, should thenceforward become chargeable to the union at large.

It is upon the foregoing provisions as to chargeability that I rely for the means of counteracting the two principal evils of property-rating, the increased temptation to clearing property by landlords, and the gradual approach to the compulsory labour system, such as existed in those parishes in England, where before the passing of the Poor Law Amendment Act the Labour Rate prevailed. In order to show the necessity of some change in the present law affecting the chargeability of paupers, it is necessary to refer to the interpretation which has been given by the law officers of the crown to the 12th section of the Poor Law Extension Act*. That section was held to have a retrospective operation, so that persons already in receipt of relief and charged to separate electoral divisions under the former Acts in force in Ireland became

* See First Annual Report of the Commissioners for administering the laws for relief of the poor in Ireland, p. 85. 8vo. edition.

chargeable to the union at large after the passing of the Poor Law Extension Act in all cases where they had not at the period of the last application for relief been resident in some one electoral division for thirty months out of the preceding three years. A reply to a further query respecting the chargeability of persons returning to the workhouse within six months from the time when they were last discharged, though somewhat ambiguous in its terms, implies that unless at the time of the new application such persons have resided for thirty months out of the preceding three years in the electoral division to which they were previously chargeable, they should be charged to the union at large.

Although these opinions have been promulgated by the Poor Law Commissioners, neither of them have been generally acted upon, and it may be held that the opportunity for a revision of the register of those receiving relief prior to the passing of the late Act has virtually lapsed, but the latter opinion has important practical consequences, which will, doubtless, before long, be perceived by those who would benefit by its application.

The extension of the period of residence necessary for chargeability provided by the late Act was intended as a protection to the towns which, under the Act of 6 and 7 Vict., cap. 92, became chargeable with the support of the rural poor

who had resided for twelve months before applying for relief, but both Acts permit an abuse
which is now likely to become common, and
which is certainly contrary to all notions of
justice. Proprietors who compel or induce the
destitute cottier tenantry upon their estates to
give up their holdings, by providing them with
the means of subsistence for six months before
applying for relief, throw the support of such
persons upon the union at large, and thus escape,
with a slender imposition, from the obligation of
supporting those whom they have deprived of
their only means of subsistence. But according
to the opinion above quoted, still readier means
exist for throwing the burden upon the union,
by inducing those who are already receiving
relief to take their discharge, and allowing them
to apply again within a few days, when they
would be chargeable to the union.

I am by no means unwilling that the support
of the permanent pauperism of Ireland should
gradually be transferred to the larger area of
unions, although such a process would in some
degree weaken the motives to careful local administration of the law; but I am quite sure that
a moderate time should be allowed to elapse
before the country can be prepared for such a
charge; and, in any case, I should wish that it
should be effected regularly and openly, rather
than by an evasion of the law, which would

generally be employed by those who least deserve
any special favour from the Legislature.

The provisions which I have proposed, would
make it impossible for an exterminating landlord
to shift from himself the burden of supporting his
own poor, except by providing them with the
means of supporting themselves for eighteen
months after they ceased to reside upon his
estate. The evils of a too stringent law of settlement would be mitigated, if not avoided altogether, by the gradual withdrawal of the permanent surplus population, who could not be
profitably employed in their own districts, from
the smaller area of taxation, and placing the
responsibility of their support upon the community.

The principle here advocated is, as far as
I know, new to Poor Law legislation. It
appears to me, after much reflection, to be sound
in theory; and if circumstances should appear
favourable to its introduction, I should wish to
see it extended to other parts of the empire.
That those who possess the chief control over
the condition of the working classes, should,
in the first place, be responsible for their support;
but that as soon as a permanent surplus is ascertained, the community should become interested
in the means of relieving their destitution,
appears to be an arrangement more equitable,

and quite as easily worked as the partial sub-
division of large areas into parishes or electoral
divisions.

I have now to consider some of the details
affecting the proposed modification of the law.
The materials for the actual sub-division of the
present electoral into rateable divisions, coter-
minous with separate estates, are nearly complete
at the present time. The Commissioners appointed to revise the boundaries of unions and
electoral divisions, have found it necessary for
their purpose to collect full materials as to
the distribution of property in Ireland, and have,
as I am informed, prepared maps, in which the
separate estates are distinguished by a distinct
colour or number. I have endeavoured to ascertain from the most competent authority, that of
intelligent clerks of unions, what amount of
practical difficulty and trouble would result from
the great increase in the number of rateable
divisions, and I have satisfied myself that this
objection is much less serious than I had in the
first instance supposed. I have been assured by
the clerk of one very large union, in which
property is much divided, that with an ordinary
assistant for the mere mechanical work, he would
have no difficulty in carrying on the proposed
system. I am, therefore, disposed to recommend
that the limit to which the sub-division should
be extended be very low:—no rateable division

containing less than one townland, or 200 statute acres.

There is some difficulty in deciding whether separate properties belonging to the same owner in one union should be united into a single rateable division, or should each be rated separately. The latter arrangement is open to an abuse which it would be very difficult to prevent or detect. The proprietor, relying upon the proposed provisions for assistance, from the union or from public funds, would be enabled to concentrate the pauperism of all his separate properties upon a single small division, and thereby to relieve himself from all taxation beyond a certain per centage of the value of that division. I am therefore of opinion that separate properties belonging to the same owner should not be formed into separate rateable divisions unless each such separate area be valued for poor-rate at not less than £.1000 per annum.

The objections to an union rate in aid of the separate rateable divisions are obvious enough. It cannot be denied that in the case of very much pauperised districts, where no practicable amount of exertion can enable the proprietor to reduce his rates below the limit, the existence of a rate in aid may make those locally interested more reckless as to further additions to the load of pauperism; but in the first place the carrying

E

of surplus rate to the account of the union does not completely relieve the local rate-payer of his share of the burden, and, after all, the practical way to consider the question, is to compare the proposed arrangement with the present system. The average area of electoral divisions throughout Ireland is about 10,000 statute acres, but in the north-eastern unions this average does not exceed 6000 acres, while in twenty of the western unions it is over 17,000 acres. With but few exceptions the present system differs but very little, in its practical working from that of union rating, except that it does not offer the same amount of convenience for administrative purposes.

There is not much reason to apprehend that the proprietors throughout Ireland, once possessed of freedom of action, will, as has been suggested, accommodate themselves passively to a maximum rate of five shillings in the pound, and leave the surplus pauperism of the poorer districts to be supported by the rest of the community. A permanent rate of that amount would necessitate a considerable change in landed property, and with such assistance at the outset as is necessary to make the continuance of any Poor Law practicable, those of the present proprietors who can command capital, or those who may succeed by purchase hereafter, will infallibly find means for the productive employment of the population, rather than submit to taxation for supporting them in idleness.

The proposition to assist emigration from public funds will be met by inquiring whence the funds for such a purpose are to be derived. It has been proposed, by extending the income-tax to Ireland, to raise funds applicable to the support of the establishment charges in connection with workhouse relief, and to the assistance of emigrants from the poorer districts. On this I will only remark, that if, upon general grounds, it appears expedient to extend direct taxation to Ireland, whether in the form of income-tax, or in the much preferable shape of a tax upon the profits of realised property, which has recently been supported by the authority of Mr. McGregor, I know of no sufficient reason for objecting to it; but I cannot conceive how those who support the union between Ireland and Great Britain, can consistently maintain that whatever expenditure is really required for remedying the complicated results of centuries of misgovernment and misconduct, which still forbid all real progress throughout a large part of this country, should be measured or limited by the amount of new taxation which it may be possible to impose. To tax Dublin or Belfast for the relief of Mayo, otherwise than in common with the rest of the empire, is to concede a principle which, if logically followed out, leads to the separation of the two countries. The only question for a consistent statesman is to ascertain whether any expenditure of public funds is absolutely required by the condition of the western districts in Ireland, and if so, how those funds may properly be applied.

It has been completely proved that the resources of many unions are utterly inadequate to the support of the present inhabitants. The people must die if they be not removed elsewhere, or supported at home out of public funds. The last plan is incompatible with good administration, and the first will not, I hope, be seriously advocated. The only remaining course is to advance sufficient funds for the removal of those whose existence where they now live reduces all around them to the level of their own misery. If, as is probable, it be possible, by the imposition of a moderate income or property-tax, to defray the interest on any sum advanced for this purpose from the Imperial Exchequer, the result will be equally advantageous to this country and the rest of the empire.

It may be objected that it is inconsistent for those who admit that there is ample scope in Ireland for the productive expenditure of capital in the reclamation and improvement of land, to advocate emigration from those very districts which, being the least improved, offer the greatest opportunities for the employment of labour. Those who argue in this way forget that a population can be maintained only out of existing resources, and that an utter excess of population directly impedes the very process through which alone future means for their support can be provided. Allowing about half-a-crown in the pound for the cost of supporting the helpless poor, the plan which I propose would leave in each district a surplus able-bodied population, whose maintenance as paupers will cost five shillings in the pound, and to support whom as independent labourers an increase of one-third in the annual value of each district relieved by emigration would be required. Under the most favourable circumstances we cannot expect a more rapid increase in the means of sustaining population.

I have now to offer a few suggestions as to some details of the present law which appear to me to demand alteration.

I have already observed that the including able-bodied widows, having more than one child, amongst the classes permanently entitled to out-door relief in the first section of the Poor Law Extension Act, is contrary to all sound principles of Poor Law legislation, inasmuch as it removes the proper inducement to industry amongst a class who are capable of contributing to production. It is, moreover, exposed to the serious practical evil of encouraging desertion. Men who would not leave their families to receive relief in the workhouse have no difficulty in so doing when they know that their wives, by representing themselves as widows, are enabled to receive relief in money or food at their own homes.

The number of persons relieved under the first section is already very formidable, amounting in some of the southern unions to 20 per cent. of the entire population*. There can be no doubt but that considerable abuses must exist in such cases, and there is no class as to which they are more easily introduced than this one of able-bodied widows.

Another and more important object is the extension of industrial schools for the education of pauper children. The value of these institutions is now generally admitted; and a strong desire for improvement in this respect exists in many parts of Ireland. The invaluable Reports of Dr. Kay Shuttleworth and Mr. Tufnell† have made the general principles which affect this question so familiar to the public, that it is not necessary to do more than to point out the

---

* This fact alone appears to me conclusive against a plan sometimes suggested, of placing the support of the helpless poor to the account of the union at large.

† Published in a separate volume by the Poor Law Commissioners.

difficulties which stand in the way of its progress. The cost of buildings suitable for a good industrial school being about twice as great as that of providing lodging for the same number of children in ordinary workhouses, the outlay for the purpose may be considered to be a sacrifice made by the present generation for the benefit of their successors ; and in this point of view the community in general may be said to be as much interested as each particular locality. It is only in places where ample means, public spirit, and intelligence co-exist that such a sacrifice will be made ; and, indeed, in the present circumstances of Ireland, it can scarcely be expected that the requisite conditions will anywhere be found. I should be prepared to support a general scheme for the extension of district industrial schools in every part of the empire; but, in any case, I think that assistance, in the form of a grant for at least one-half of the cost of the construction of the requisite buildings, would be highly advantageous to the future progress of this country, and be amply repaid by the improved industry and morality of those who, by no fault of theirs, have been from their birth deprived of every favourable influence.

One further suggestion I have to offer as to one of the best grounded complaints against the working of the present Poor Law. It is notorious that the valuation of rateable property, which serves as the basis of taxation for relief of the poor, has generally been performed in the most defective manner, owing in part to the want of skill or corrupt bias of the persons employed as valuators, and in part to the necessary absence of any uniform principle amongst persons chosen at random from various classes of the community. The instances of inequality and consequent injustice are so frequent as to make this evil a characteristic of the present taxation. The only effectual remedy will be found in the completion of the general valuation of Ireland, and its adaptation to the purposes of Poor Law rating. Various causes have tended to retard the conclusion of this most important work. The time of Mr. Griffith, under whose direction and control the operations have been placed, has been largely interfered with by the exigencies of other branches of the public service, for which his talents and experience have been demanded; and it is believed that the staff placed at his disposal might be considerably increased with a corresponding advantage in hastening the completion of the work. I believe that all those practically concerned in the administration of this country will agree that there is no single way in which public funds may more profitably be expended than this, and, as I shall presently point out, a considerable proportion of the staff employed may be permanently retained with advantage to the public service. The principle of valuation by competent public officers being conceded, it may be hoped that it will not again be abandoned, and that provision will be made for the periodic revision of such valuation. A very important proviso, the absence of which is felt as a material check to agricultural improvement, would be the exemption of lands reclaimed, or improved by thorough drainage from re-valuation, until the expiration of five or seven years from the commencement of the improvements. Under the existing system the increase of taxation frequently precedes the increase of production consequent upon improvements, and the proprietor is forced at the same time to repay the cost of the work without any increase to his means.

The necessity of amendment in the present Poor Law being the subject which most urgently demands the attention of the Legislature, and with respect to which public opinion is most unsettled, I have been induced to enter into details which must have wearied most of my readers. I shall pass more lightly over the other topics which remain to be noticed, not because I underrate their importance, but that they either present less practical difficulty, or that I feel myself less competent to discuss their details.

First in order, as being connected with the object of security for the investment of capital in agriculture, is the necessity of providing compensation for improvements effected by the tenant. The measure which passed the House of Commons during the last session is so superior to those which preceded it that I shall keep it principally in view in the few remarks which I have to offer on the subject.

Every one who has attempted to devise a measure for regulating and assuring the mutual rights of landlords and tenants has felt the extreme difficulty of legal interference on a subject which, in a well-regulated state of society, should be arranged by an equitable contract between the two parties. But it is precisely because the relations between landlord and tenant in Ireland have been upon the worst possible footing, that a law assuring to each his just rights is the indispensable preliminary to the existence of equitable voluntary arrangements, and for this purpose one of the foremost provisions of such a measure, should be to sanction and facilitate such voluntary agreements. To accomplish the direct objects of the law it should make the machinery as simple and speedy in its operation as possible, and on this ground the intervention of a responsible public officer, whose decision should be final and binding upon all parties, appears to me almost indispensable to the success of the measure; the possibility of incurring expense in litigation would make it absolutely a dead letter. Concurring in most of the provisions of the Bill of last session as, in its amended form, it passed the House of Commons, 1 may express the earnest hope that another year may not pass without satisfying the claims of justice and sound policy which have so long awaited an equitable adjustment of this question. Although the diminished competition for land must at the present time materially lessen the power hitherto possessed by landlords, yet, with the experience of the past, we cannot expect to see tenants generally disposed to invest additional capital and labour in improvements so long as the state of law shall make it still possible for a proprietor to deprive them of the fruits of enterprise by increasing rent, or by removing them from their holdings without any equivalent compensation.

The Encumbered Estates Act of last session will, it is generally believed, be found much less efficacious in its operation than was expected by those who supported that important measure. The subject is so closely connected with the whole state of the laws affecting the transfer of real property, that it is impossible to consider it separately; and it has already been found in practice that it will fail to accomplish the objects which it was the policy of that Act to promote, without a thorough revision and an extensive reform of that branch of the law. A topic so vast, so complicated in its bearings, and so difficult in its practical details, would require a considerable treatise for its thorough discussion; it will be sufficient for me to recapitulate the principal objects which it should be the aim of such a reform to achieve.

*First.* A complete system of national registration, as well for the purpose of ascertaining and finally settling the title to land held in fee, as for simplifying the record of all legal transactions affecting it, whether of the nature of conveyance or incumbrance.

*Secondly.* The removal or considerable diminution of taxation affecting leases or sales of landed property.

*Thirdly.* The simplification of the complicated tenures by which land is held in Ireland, giving a power to the tenant to convert certain tenures into perpetuities at an equitable rent, and to purchase the fee by the redemption of such quit rents.

*Fourthly.* The limitation of the power of *tying up land* by legal process in such a manner as to prevent its sale or conveyance, with due security to the rights of all parties having legal or equitable claims to the *property represented by such land.*

If it be really believed that the introduction of capital and skill are indispensable to permanent improvement in the impoverished districts of Ireland, there is no possibility of further postponing measures, without which that change cannot be accomplished. Making all due allowance for the time really required for maturing good practical measures, it will be felt hereafter that any Government which shall allow the fear of opposition, the representations of interested parties, or the mere reluctance to encounter a difficult subject to delay the settlement of this question, will have grievously failed in the performance of their duty to this country. I cannot but hope that such will not be the case with the present Government, when I find that most of the measures above enumerated have been supported by the eminent authority of Sir Charles Trevelyan, in his " Irish Crisis," to which I have already referred.

It has been the less necessary for me to enter at length into this branch of my subject, as the public must be, to a great extent, convinced of the necessity for considerable changes in the law, through the publications of such practical and competent writers as Mr. Jonathan Pim, Mr. Pierce Mahony, and Mr. Booth. I believe that the majority of the intelligent landowners in this country are by this time fully persuaded that their own real interest will be better served by a course of legislation which would tend to accelerate improvement, than by a fruitless attempt to prop up the present tottering system, in which a large portion of the land of this country is retained in the hands of men who are unable to make it serviceable to themselves or to the community. I am persuaded that the alarmists, who threaten a general confiscation of landed property as the result of any useful change in the law, very much exaggerate the results which would in reality be produced. Many must, doubtless, consent to a sacrifice of some portion of their apparent position; but in most cases the growth of national prosperity would far more than counterbalance the seeming loss, by substituting a real for a nominal income, and genuine independence of circumstances for fictitious importance.

In connection with this subject I will notice a claim occasionally made by embarrassed proprietors for the imposition of a portion of Poor Law taxation upon mortgagees and persons deriving income under family settlements. With respect to the first-named parties the proposition is clearly unjust. There is no assignable reason for taxing mortgagees who do not exercise any of the rights of property otherwise than in common with all other members of the community. As well might it be proposed to authorise the payers of poor-rate to deduct a proportion of the rate from their tradesmen's bills.

With respect, however, to family charges the case is different. These charges were created with reference to the value of the estate at the period of settlement; and it certainly appears

unjust that nearly the entire proceeds of an estate
should, as now happens, be payable to parties
who were merely intended to enjoy a moderate
proportion of the income arising from it. There
is some difficulty in devising a mode of fairly
adjusting this question, since the rental commonly
exceeds the valuation for Poor Law purposes;
and, therefore, the landlord should not be entitled
to deduct a poundage-rate equal to the actual
deduction from his income as compared with the
valuation. I am inclined to propose that any
proprietor of rateable property, liable to pay an
annual sum charged upon such property to any
person not having given valuable consideration
for the same, should be entitled to deduct from
each pound sterling two-thirds of the poundage-
rate, which, if assessed upon the annual value of
the said property according to the valuation then
in force in the Union, would equal the amount of
poor-rate actually paid in respect to the said
property by the said proprietor, as shown by
receipts from the collector, or deducted from rent
payable to him by tenants, as shown by the
tenants' receipts.

The subjects of Emigration and Colonization
are altogether too extensive to be discussed in
these pages. I have been forced to anticipate
some observations, which I should have made at
this point, when speaking of the absolute necessity of relieving over-population by the removal

of those who cannot be supported from the existing resources of certain districts. The propriety of providing immediate employment in the colonies, upon useful public works, for a portion of the destitute able-bodied population who would emigrate if assisted in the manner which I have proposed, should necessarily be considered in connection with any public measure for promoting emigration. So much information has recently been given to the public by the publication of the evidence taken before the Committees House of Lords, which sat in 1847 and 1848, and by the pamphlets of such men as Sir Randolph Routh, Mr. Godley, &c. that the facts and the general principles involved must be familiar to most of my readers. I think it proper, however, to notice the chief objection which is made to any assistance from public funds being applied to this object. It is known that the number of emigrants from Irish ports in 1847, was 95,952, and it is believed from 40,000 to 50,000 Irish emigrants sailed from English ports, making a total number of about 140,000 who left Ireland in that year; and it is expected that the returns for the present year will even exceed that number. With these data it is argued that the present rate for emigration is as great as the circumstances either of Ireland or the colonies demand; that the result of giving any assistance from public funds would be actually to diminish the present flow of population

from Ireland, by leading all classes to seek the
means of transport from that source, rather than
from their own savings or sacrifices. This mode
of viewing the question utterly loses sight of the
conditions under which alone emigration is desirable or profitable to this country. What we
require is not less population, but more capital.
The only reason for sending away what we now
call surplus inhabitants is, that in our poorer
districts there do not exist means for giving them
productive employment, and that there is no
reasonable prospect, so long as they continue
to overcrowd the labour market that capital will
flow in, and render those parts of Ireland capable
of sustaining in comforts a population equal to
that which now dwells there in squalid misery.

On the other hand, it is important that too
much should not be expected from emigration as
a means for the improvement of Ireland. In
districts where there still exists enterprise and
capital, the removal of the nests of pauperism
which have grown round most of the towns and
larger villages, and which, under the operation
of the Poor Law, are rapidly absorbing the
existing resources, will frequently be a direct
source of prosperity. But in the poorer parts
of the west of Ireland emigration will, of itself,
be but of small service, except to the individuals
whom it may rescue from their present idle,
degraded, and half-starved condition. Those

F

districts will be merely brought back to the condition in which a great part of Ireland remained for centuries, with a thin population, little agricultural skill, and no capital. Emigration is indeed an indispensable preliminary, but if not accompanied by measures which will give security for the investment of capital, whether by proprietors or tenant farmers, and remove the obstacles which now retard or prevent its influx, no permanent improvement can be expected.

I have, throughout the preceding pages, abstained from any allusion to a measure which has been most earnestly recommended by some of those who have laboured to forward the progress of improvement in Ireland. I allude to the reclamation of waste lands by the State. I had myself, to a great extent, shared the opinions of those who were disposed to place confidence in that proposal; but I confess that inquiry and further consideration have led me to doubt its efficacy. The circumstances which determine the profitableness of such an investment of capital are not susceptible of easy or immediate calculation, and it is quite clear that if the undertaking be not profitable, it would be a waste of the national funds to devote them to the purpose. It is most probable that if the obstacles which now prevent the application of capital to the land be removed, a considerable extent of reclamation will gradually be effected in those localities where it will be attended with advantage. But it is doubted by those most competent to decide such a question, whether at the present time any extensive tracts of waste land could be reclaimed at a cost which would remunerate an ordinary capitalist for his outlay.

As it is not impossible, however, that attempts may be made by individuals or companies to improve or reclaim districts now little populated, I should be disposed to suggest that the provisions above recommended, as to emigration from over-populated districts, should be extended to internal migration or home colonization, by giving authority to Boards of Guardians, and to the Poor Law Commissioners, to advance a certain sum per head as outfit to parties undertaking the reclamation of waste lands, upon their constructing approved habitations for immigrant labourers.

The propriety of the completion by the State of general arterial drainage, and other works which would facilitate the reclamation or improvement of land, such as deepening streams, &c. is a question quite independent of that above noticed, and appears to me to be recommended by the soundest policy.

A measure, not indeed universal in its application, but yet urgently called for by the condition of many extensive districts, is a reform in the management of property under the Court of Chancery. If it has at length been decided that the Legislature shall take cognizance of the duties connected with the possession of property, and shall as far as possible secure their performance, it is not too much to expect that where the rights of property devolve upon its own creatures, it should cease to permit so scandalous a neglect of those duties as is inevitable under the existing system of administration. Amongst the many varieties of misery which this country presents, I can assert, from extensive observation, that properties placed under the management of Courts of Equity display the most uniform of hopeless spectacles of wretchedness and neglect.

In the preceding pages I have freely stated my opinion that nothing less than the concurrence of a number of remedial measures, appropriate to the numerous evils which affect the state of Ireland, can be of any real service towards her recovery from her present condition ; unfortunately, I am well aware that the temper of the times, the character of our leading statesmen, the very genius of our form of Government, are all unfavourable to so great an effort of legislation as that which our circumstances require.

If my voice could have any weight at this conjucture, I would earnestly adjure those who have the responsibility of directing our destiny calmly

to view our condition, and to see whether a great
and unusual effort is not required to achieve
a victory over the delays and impediments by
which measures of acknowledged utility are
retarded, until they cease to be of any practical
value. In time of peace it may be safe to proceed slowly and unequally in arranging the
details of military preparation, but when the
enemy is in the field, a General who satisfies
himself with attending to any single portion
of his duties, or neglects to provide for the
subsistence or clothing of his troops, the conveyance of his artillery, protection for his bag-
gage, or any other essential to safety and success,
is rightly pronounced incompetent to fill his
high position, and unworthy of the confidence of
his country. In the present circumstances of
Ireland, it is not enough to propose or to promise
useful changes—they must be accomplished, and
that speedily, if she is to be preserved from utter
ruin and confusion.

The most pressing and prominent evils of this
country are those connected with economical
and social causes; I have, therefore, felt myself justified in considering them apart from
the other causes which affect our position, and
which have so long disturbed and agitated the
public mind. I should not, however, deal
fairly with my readers, if I allowed them to
suppose that these are of no importance, or that

they will not demand further legislative interference. The false principles by which the
Government of Ireland has so long been guided,
and from which the entire empire has reaped such
bitter fruits, have been for the most part abjured
and abandoned; but if England will not continue
to suffer from her misdeeds, she must complete
the work of justice. That great reparation,
which was commenced in 1829, must be followed
on to its legitimate conclusion; perfect equality
of legal rights and religious faith must be
thoroughly and practically acknowledged; then,
and not until then, that progress towards prosperity and contentment can commence, which
Time, the healer of the evils of the past, alone
can lead to the desired consummation.

———

P. S.—Since the above pages were written, I
have seen a copy of Resolutions passed at a
general meeting of Poor Law Guardians, in
Dublin, which appear to a considerable extent
to agree with the recommendations herein contained. Having been written for the most part
in the country, it is probable that I may have
omitted to notice several of the most recent publications on the subjects herein alluded to.

# APPENDIX.

———◆———

## APPENDIX, A.

*Extracts from a Letter addressed to the* Right Honourable Henry Labouchere, *Chief Secretary for Ireland, by* William Monsell, Esq., *dated September* 18, 1846.

\* \* \* \* \*

It is but very lately that our real position has been known. When the provisions of the 9th and 10th Victoria, c. 107, were arranged by the Government, they did not foresee that before the 1st of September the rot among the potatoes would be making fearful ravages in every electoral division in Ireland; that in a number of electoral divisions there would not be a potato fit to eat upon the 1st of October; and that there probably would not remain any potatoes available for human food in any part of Ireland upon the 1st of November.

\* \* \* \* \*

I have already shown the magnitude of the sum which must be expended for the present year. We are probably entering upon a series of years of distress. The money necessary for the support of the Irish people during their transition from one sort of food to another, must—at all events a very large proportion of it must—be raised from the land. If this sum, paid by the land, does not revolve back again upon the land, if this " secretion be not again

" absorbed into the mass of blood," it will be impossible for the nation to recover the shock.

     \*     \*     \*     \*     \*

I repeat that in every corner of Ireland, in every barony, almost in every townland, the money expended upon its improvement would return a large interest. In drainage alone millions might be so expended that they would return an interest of at least 10 per cent (the usual estimate made by practical men is higher, but I am anxious to avoid exaggeration), and the capital of the country would be, of course, largely increased by such an expenditure. In proportion to the increase or decrease of capital will be the increase or decrease of the demand for labour; and as all that our poor require to make them prosperous and happy is employment, every measure for Ireland is mischievous or beneficial in proportion as it increases or diminishes the means of giving them employment. An increasing capital will employ more labour—a decreasing capital, less.

     \*     \*     \*     \*     \*

Every occupier of land who pays for a useless and unprofitable work will be less able next year to give employment than he is now, by the precise amount which he is rated for such work; while the expenditure of the same sum, so assessed upon profitable improvement of his land, would enable him to employ next year a larger number of labourers than he can now do, by the exact amount of increase to his income which would be derived from such improvement. And it is very important here to remark that not only would he be enabled to employ more labour, but the present circumstances of the country would induce him to do so. The farmers are all asking what they shall grow next year in place of potatoes. They must leave their land idle or adopt a new mode of husbandry, and this improved husbandry will involve an increase of labour. If their capital is to be diminished, not increased, how are their fields to be tilled ? This, then, is the first evil of the existing Act, that it involves the expenditure of vast sums of money to be torn out of the already small capital of this country, on unproductive labour—that it will increase the disproportion already existing between capital and labour, and perpetuate misery by taking away the means of giving employment.

This plan has certainly its apt parallel in the conduct of the youth who spends, during his first university term, a considerable portion of his patrimony ; and as the hand of ruin is gently laid upon him by silky tradesmen, who promise him a long day for the payment of his bill, so also this unproductive expenditure is rendered more tolerable, although not less certain, in its operation, by its being made with borrowed money.

*    *    *    *    *

It is, for these reasons, perfectly certain that public works are not a satisfactory way to give to the destitute that employment they require. There is a place in which they are eminently useful. They must be used as a means, not as an end—as a screw to enforce the employment of labour in a profitable way. The Government cannot, by Act of Parliament, compel drainage or fencing ; but they can compel the owners of land to employ the poor, and make those who refuse to employ them on productive labour, pay for their employment on public works. There must be some impulse besides public spirit to put a large proportion of those who ought to exert themselves into motion, and unfortunately there is no stimulus which is so universal in its operation as self-interest. This, then, brings me to another objection to the new Act, *viz.* that it makes no difference between the improving landlord and the man who either neglects his duty at home, or, in some distant land, consumes the produce of those hereditary possessions upon which he has never bestowed a thought. It is a dead flat—an equality of injustice ;

or, if there be any inequality in it, it is not in favour of, but against the improving landowner.

*   *   *   *

Therefore, this simple level of taxation is a direct penalty inflicted by the State on improvements. The one man has made his tenants comfortable, and few of them require relief, the other has ground them to the earth, and they are starving; and the first is to contribute more towards the support of his neighbour's poor—the poor whom his neighbour, by his own misconduct, has created—than their own landlord does; for the one pays a cess merely on rent—the other, on rent and capital expended. Surely such a system is as impolitic as it is unjust. The prosperity of every country is very much involved in the conduct of the wealthy and the powerful. You ought, therefore, to encourage, urge, assist the improving landlord, and not tax him for those who neglect their duties; you should endeavour to drive the negligent, indolent, or hard-hearted landowner " into his " duties or out of his position."

If the man who has spent his time and his money on the amelioration of the condition of his dependants is to be taxed for the support of those who have spent neither the one nor the other upon anything but self-gratification, you will compel him to give up his improvements. You will take away from him, not perhaps the disposition, but the power to carry them on. He cannot support the whole of his own and half his neighbour's poor. He must, therefore, allow them all to go upon the public works, and to be supported by the public purse; and what will be the effect—the effect both physical and moral—of such injustice? It is the office of Government to prevent evil. By this means they would encourage it; and however true it may be that they can do little positive good, they would at all events show their power of doing a great deal of positive harm. But it may be said what are Government to do? If they exempt well-managed estates from the support of the poor who inhabit ill-managed estates, who will support them ? A badly managed, over-populated property will not be able to support its own poor. Well, who is responsible for the bad management of any property besides the individual to whom it belongs? Certainly not the owner of the neighbouring property. He has not had the slightest control over it. He has had nothing to say to the direction or education of its proprietor. He has not directly or indirectly had any power over him ; and without power there can be no responsibility.

I do not wish to allude even to what are usually called politics ; but yet I cannot help saying that for the misdeeds of such a proprietor, the governing powers of the country are, to say the least of it, far more responsible than any other person or persons. Laws educate ; it was the Government that made the laws, and the sort of education which a few years ago they gave, did not certainly tend to foster any proper notion of responsibility in the breasts of those who were brought up under them. But the old laws have given place to wiser and better ones. Government has repented. True ; but there are two parts of repentance—amendment of life, and restitution. The exercise of the former does not dispense with the necessity of the latter. It does, therefore, seem to me that justice and the interests of the community would be far better consulted by giving some assistance out of the Consolidated Fund to over-peopled miserable properties, than by over-taxing the benevolent landlord, whose property happens to be contiguous to them, throwing those at present receiving regular employment out of work. This, then, is a most serious evil in the plan under our consideration. It taxes alike those who do their duty, and those who, by neglecting it, increase the amount of destitution. Such appears to me to be some of the most objectionable features of the existing measure for relieving distress :—

1. Unproductive work, to be executed by borrowed money.

2. The demoralisation of the people, by congregating them in large masses on public works.

3. The diversion of one-fourth of the money to be raised from the relief of the destitute.

4. The taxing improving landowners and occupiers for the sins of those who neglect their duty.

As there is some truth in Jeremy Bentham's remark, that no one has a right to object to any existing system who has not got a better to suggest in its place, I shall now take the liberty of again urging upon your notice the plan I laid before you last week; and I may just remark that the fact of this plan, in its main outlines, having suggested itself, at the same time and without communication with one another, to some persons of intelligence in the county of Limerick; to the writer of the well-considered resolutions adopted in the county of Meath; and to Mr. Ball, who superintended last year the Relief Committees in the south of Ireland; may be taken, perhaps, as some slight presumption in favour of its wisdom and feasibility. I will now insert the paper I submitted to you, and then proceed to point out the advantages which it appears to me to possess over the existing law.

" As it is desirable that the sums of money to be spent on
" the relief of the poor should be applied to productive
" labour, it is suggested that after the holding of the
" present sessions in any barony or district, and after the
" probable sum of money required to employ the poor in
" such barony or district for some months be ascertained,
" such sums be forthwith applotted on the owners and
" occupiers of land in each district, according to the Poor
" Law valuation.

" That such applotment be placed at the next police
" barrack, within the district, for three days, for the

" information of all cess-payers who may wish to see it;
" and that notice of its being so placed be posted on the
" usual place for posting notices in the district."

" That it shall be lawful for any persons representing at
" least three-fourths of the taxation of any townland, or
" number of contiguous townlands associating themselves
" together, to require the sum to be levied off such town-
" land or townlands, to be spent in productive works, and
" that such works, upon being approved of by the Board
" of Works, be executed by their officer; and that the
" wages of labourers employed on them be paid by the
" pay-clerk of the district, under the same regulations as
" are laid down for public works."

" That the officer of the Board of Works, at his discre-
" tion, employ on such works the persons recommended to
" him by the district Relief Committee, and none others;
" and that such works be, as far as possible, laid out in
" task-work."

" That the Board of Works be authorised, upon such
" arrangements being made, to postpone such portion of
" the public works, recommended by the Presentment
" Sessions, as they shall see fit; and to expend the portion
" of the money presented on any townland, in carrying out
" the requisition from such townland."

You will observe that these suggestions agree with the
enactments of the 10th Victoria in every particular except
one, and that one is, the application of the money raised.
This plan proposes to raise the same sum from the same persons.
It places the execution of works and payment of labourers
in the same hands. But instead of setting these labourers
to work on unproductive works, it employs them on profitable labour. It returns to the land what it takes from it,
only taking care that in its way, what is so taken may
relieve the destitute. It confers a benefit upon the landowner
and farmer, because it improves their property; and while
with one hand it takes money out of their pockets, with the

other it gives them the means to pay it. It confers a benefit upon the labourer, because it provides him with work near his own home; because it does not demoralise him, by placing him with large masses, where the evil-disposed so often give the tone to the whole lot; and because it gives him a better chance than he otherwise could have of being regularly employed in future years. It gets over the difficulty of finding competent stewards to place over the works, because it makes it the interest of every occupier of land to see the work on his land properly executed. It insures the expenditure of the whole amount of money to be raised for the relief of the destitute, because the work which it contemplates requires no purchase of land, and very little horse work or blasting.

\* \* \* \* \*

Never since the connection of Ireland with England, has so awful a power been placed in the hands of any statesman as in yours. The whole country is, as it were, fused to your hands. On you depends the future shape which it will assume. If you use your opportunities well—if you develop its resources—if you increase its capital—if you improve its agriculture—if you distribute its wealth as it ought to be distributed, its progress in the next two or three years will be greater than the progress ever made by any country in the same time.

If you take the easy course—if you throw away the opportunity placed by Providence in your hands—if you allow the vast sums, of which you have to direct the distribution, to be spent unproductively, we shall retrograde as fast as under the other alternative we should have advanced; and those who have been year after year hoping against hope, and labouring against the tide, will fold their hands in despair.

I am, my dear Sir, &c.,

WILLIAM MONSELL.

# APPENDIX, B.

*To His Excellency* The Earl of BESBOROUGH, *Lord Lieutenant-General and General Governor of Ireland, &c., &c., &c.*

*The Memorial of the Undersigned Proprietors and Occupiers of Land in Ireland.*

HUMBLY SHOWETH,

THAT your Memorialists received with great satisfaction the announcement contained in Mr. Secretary Labouchere's Letter, of the 5th October last, to the Chairman of the Board of Public Works, that your Excellency was prepared to give a more extended operation to the Act for the Employment of the labouring poor of this country, than was contemplated by the original provisions of that law.

That with a view of availing themselves of the construction which your Excellency appeared thus prepared to sanction, your Memorialists directed their immediate attention to the introduction of the system of reproductive works into their respective districts, but they regret to be compelled to state, that, for one or more of the following reasons, they are of opinion that in the majority of cases it is impossible to carry out your Excellency's views in the manner directed by Mr. Labouchere's Letter :—

1st.—Because it is scarcely possible to discover works of such universal benefit as will render them profitable or reproductive to all the inhabitants of any electoral division.

2nd.—Because, by the terms of Mr. Labouchere's Letter, drainage, in connection with subsoiling, appears to be the only work of a private character, authorised as a substitute for public works ; whereas, in many districts of Ireland, thorough drainage is not required, though subsoiling may be carried on advantageously, while in others works of a totally different character, such as clearing, fencing, or the making of farm roads, are the chief works to which labour could at present be most beneficially applied.

3rd.—Because in cases of works, the cost of which is to be made an exclusive charge on the lands to be improved, as specified in paragraph No. 4 of Mr. Labouchere's Letter, it is necessary to the just operation of the system, that each and every proprietor should undertake his own proportion of the sum to which the electoral division is assessed; and this unanimity it is seldom possible to attain for various reasons, which will occur to all practical persons. The number of electoral divisions in Ireland is about 2050, representing, according to the Ordnance survey, about 60,000 townlands chiefly in the hands of separate proprietors, being upon an average about 30 townlands to each electoral division; of these many are in the hands of absentees, whose consent it is almost impossible to obtain; others may be of unsound mind, or infants; more may be strict tenants for life, in which cases there are many difficulties and impediments to obtaining the required guarantee; whilst others may be in such embarrassed circumstances, that the whole rental of their property may be absorbed in payment of interest money and expenses; or a few proprietors may prefer a public road to private works, and by their opposition counteract the wishes of the majority for the adoption of reproductive works in their electoral division. Any of these causes would, in the opinion of your Memorialists, either render inoperative the relaxation of the law contemplated by your Excellency, or so embarrass the proceedings of those who choose to avail themselves of its provisions as to render their efforts for that purpose totally unavailing.

Your Memorialists are indeed well aware that by the interpretation given to Mr. Labouchere's Letter, if a portion only of the assessment on an electoral division

is expended on reproductive works, the general amount of
rate will be thereby reduced ; but they submit to your Excellency, that, in practice, this will seldom if ever be carried
out, because it cannot be expected that a proprietor will
submit both to the direct charge incurred for drainage or
other improvement of his property (which, it must be
remembered, is imposed solely for the sake of employing
the destitute poor) and likewise to that proportion of the
general rate which is cast upon him by the refusal of other
proprietors to undertake their own share. Such a state of
things would not only involve the enterprising proprietor in
a double expense, but would, in precisely the same proportion, relieve his negligent neighbour from his allotted share
of the burden.

To obviate these difficulties, and to carry out the principle
which your Excellency has so wisely recognised, that the
amount of taxation necessary to meet the present emergency
shall be expended upon reproductive works, your Memorialists respectfully submit, that each proprietor who may be
willing to charge his proportion of the rate for employing
the poor upon any particular land to be improved thereby,
shall be entitled to have it expended on his own land, and be
relieved to that extent from the payment of rate; and that
the works so to be undertaken shall not be confined to
drainage or subsoiling, but shall include all works of a
reproductive nature, suited to the wants of the locality
for which they are proposed, provided only that such works
meet with the approbation of the Board of Public Works.

Your Memorialists humbly beg to remind your Excellency, that in this request they but seek to avail themselves
of your Excellency's benevolent intentions, without the
necessity of a combined movement on the part of every
proprietor in an electoral division. That by these suggestions the details of the system are not by any means rendered
more complicated or difficult, but, on the contrary, that the

adoption of townlands, in preference to electoral divisions, will be found in practice more simple and easy, and in its results productive of this great advantage, that it will turn the current of labour back into its legitimate channels.

Your Memorialists, therefore, humbly but earnestly pray your Excellency to enlarge the terms by which your Excellency's intentions are at present limited, and to declare, " That any townland which shall expend in labour upon " drainage or other productive works its proportion of the " sum assessed on the barony in which it is situated, shall " be exempt from further taxation on that behalf."

And your Memorialists, as in duty bound, will ever pray.

## APPENDIX, C.

### OBSERVATIONS AND SUGGESTIONS

*On the Subject of the Present Question of Taxation under the Poor Law Extension Act for Ireland, submitted to the consideration of his Excellency the* Earl of CLARENDON, *Lord Lieutenant-General and Governor of Ireland.*

By WILLIAM TALBOT CROSBIE, Esq., D. L., *Ardfert Abbey, County of Kerry.*

WHILE it is a matter of dispute whether the labouring class of Ireland are not too numerous to find profitable employment in the ordinary occupations of agriculture, supposing the whole available land of Ireland to be brought into full cultivation—that is, where nothing further is required than is the case in a farm in the highest state of improvement, namely, to plough and manure the land, put in the crops, and reap their produce—it is quite indis-

putable that for some years to come, in order to bring
the land to that desirable state, there can be found full and
profitable occupation for all the able-bodied labourers of
that part of the kingdom. For all the most necessary and
expensive of such works of reclamation and improvement
the Legislature have agreed to provide the landed proprietors
with funds by loan, on terms the most advantageous; and
though the amount to which such loans are limited is small,
compared to the requirements of the country, it can hardly be
doubted that, in the present calamitous state of Ireland,
Government would be ready to extend this very judicious aid
to any amount that might be necessary for the development
of its resources. Under these circumstances, with profitable
employment for the labourer at hand, and money provided
to pay for such employment, it would appear difficult to
believe that the landed property of Ireland is weighed down
—in some cases nearly confiscated—by a tax for supporting
the able-bodied poor in a state of the most demoralising
idleness; such is, nevertheless, the case. It is notorious that
though the amount of loan above alluded to as granted by
the Legislature has been applied for, yet the works for which
it was intended have not been carried on so rapidly or
zealously as might have been expected. And it is quite
certain that were a further amount sanctioned by Parliament, proprietors would not be found to any considerable
extent prepared to avail themselves of it.

As to the cause of this apparently unaccountable state of
things, there is in this country scarcely a second opinion.
There is no man practically acquainted with the country and
the working of the Poor Law, who will not assign the
unjust pressure caused by the present area of taxation as the
chief cause of this anomalous state of things. As the law
stands at present, the proprietor who performs his duty
to the full, employing every able-bodied labourer on his
estate, fails to relieve himself from rate, except in the same

degree in which he relieves every idle proprietor in the same electoral division : it is quite right that he should bear his proportion of the expense of the helpless class, and of the workhouse establishment; but that, having employed all his own labourers, he should pay for the support of the able-bodied poor in the remainder of the electoral division, in the same proportion as those other proprietors who have neglected their duty, appears to me most unjust, and, as long as such a grievance exists, it must naturally act as a heavy discouragement to those who are disposed to exert themselves. This injustice cannot be more forcibly illustrated than in the case of Mr. St. John Blacker :—

"This gentleman, on his estate in the county of Kerry, in "the Listowel Union, laid out between the December 1, "1847, and September 16, 1848, a sum of £.2810 15s. 9d. "in works of improvement; this was paid to labourers, of "whom he employed from 280 to 300 daily, exclusive of "what was paid for implements, and to overseers—exclusive, "also, of a tilery, at which twenty-five hands were employed. "Yet, notwithstanding this very considerable outlay, and his "having employed all the labourers on his own property, and "a large number from other lands, he has, during the same "period, been subjected to three rates, amounting together to "11s. 10d. in the pound." Nor can I more strongly contrast the evils which arise from the placing it beyond the power of any proprietor to relieve himself by his exertions, and the advantages which result from enabling him to do so, than by stating what actually took place in the adjoining electoral divisions of Ardfert and Abbeydorney. In the summer of 1847, under the operations of the " Temporary Relief Act," the proprietor* of almost the entire of the latter electoral division succeeded, by means of combination with his tenants, and by mutual exertion, in employing all the able-bodied poor of this district; so that the amount of gratuitous

---

* The Proprietor is Mr. Crosbie, the writer of this Paper.

relief in that division required only for the support of
the helpless poor, employment having been provided for the
able-bodied, was but at the rate of 1s. 6d. per pound on the
valuation, raised by subscription and voluntary assessment:
whereas, in the division of Ardfert, managed by the same
Relief Committee, the same proprietor, holding but a comparatively small portion of it, having failed in effecting a
similar combination of exertion with the owners and occupiers of this electoral division, gratuitous relief amounted, in
consequence, to a rate of 5s. 7d. in the pound. To remedy
the state of things here described, many suggestions have
been made, of which two only have been seriously advocated,
namely :—

1st. To make townlands the area of taxation instead of
electoral divisions.

2nd. To constitute, wherever practicable, individual properties into electoral divisions; and where this was not
possible, to combine two or more properties similarly circumstanced, and where owners were anxious to act in conjunction,
into one electoral division.

There is no doubt that either of the foregoing projects
would remedy the evil here complained of; but there appears
to be so much difficulty in carrying out either, and so many
counterbalancing objections have been raised to them, if
even practicable, that I have, after the best consideration I
could give the matter, endeavoured to frame these suggestions, with a view to insure in a great degree the same effects,
and to avoid the greater part of the objections made to the
former proposed changes. As far as I have been able to
gather, the objections made to townland taxation are chiefly
the following :—

1st. The immense amount of detail required for each union
to keep distinct accounts for every townland, which in some
instances consist of only a few acres.

2nd. The want of unity of action and purpose where a
union was split up into such very minute divisions.

3rd. The impossibility of representing at the Board of Guardians (with whom rests the power of taxation) such small divisions.

4th. The undue advantage given to the townlands from which the population had been cleared, or to farms merely devoted to grazing purposes.

5th. The direct inducement to such clearing of townlands, commonly called extermination.

To the second proposition, *viz.*, to make a property, or two or more combining properties, into electoral divisions, it is thought, generally speaking, this is impracticable, from the way in which properties are scattered and intersected—and, if practicable, it would be open to several of the objections above detailed, as well as to some peculiar to itself. For instance, we will suppose the case—on an extensive property an industrious tenant occupying a townland, and employing all his labourers, and surrounded by other tenants who did nothing, and with an absentee and unimproving landlord; this tenant, notwithstanding his exertions, would have to pay the heavy rate applicable to the entire estate. In lieu therefore of either of the above propositions, I would suggest that in every electoral division there be two rates—the first for the expenses and maintenance of the establishment and the helpless class—that this rate be as at present levied off the entire electoral division, without any power of exemption.

That there be a second rate for the support of the able-bodied for the first six months; this rate to be also levied on the entire electoral division, estimated sufficient to support all the able-bodied paupers for that period.

That previous to striking all future rates the books of the electoral division be examined, and any townland not appearing to have furnished any able-bodied for relief during the previous six months, to be deducted from the gross valuation of the division on which the estimated amount required for the able-bodied for the next six months is to be assessed, and to be exempted from all shares of this rate.

For example, we will suppose an electoral division to consist of ten townlands, A, B, C, D, E, F, G, H, I, K, each valued at £.200, making a total of £.2000; that an amount of £.400 is estimated as necessary for the able-bodied for the next six months, and a rate is about to be struck: as the law stands at present, this would be assessed on the entire division valued at £.2000, making a rate of four shillings in the pound; but if, on examining the books for the previous half year, it be found that no able-bodied paupers have been relieved from the townlands C and D, then their amount, £.400, to be deducted from the gross valuation of the electoral division, and the amount required, £.400, to be assessed on the remaining townlands valued at £.1600; C and D would then be exempt, and the remainder of the electoral division would be subject to a 5s. rate. If in any case the rate on the electoral division, or rather on the unexempted portion of it, exceed a certain amount, say 7s. in the £.1, then a rate in aid to be levied off the whole electoral division, without any power of exemption; if again, an electoral division, or any part thereof, become liable to a certain rate, say 10s. per £.1, then a rate in aid to be levied off the union at large *. Towns to be provided for by making them, where the population exceeds, say 1000, an electoral division of themselves; and when their rate exceeds the average of the union, which average shall be calculated as if the rate were on the entire net annual value of each electoral division, without exemption of any townland, then that a rate in aid be levied off the union at large.

That whereas (as the law now stands) a pauper removed from an electoral division, to which he was fairly chargeable, can, by being kept for six months from off the books, be placed

---

* If an income-tax be possible, I should prefer this as a remedy for such a case as a district requiring such an exorbitant rate.

after that period on the union at large, instead of against the electoral division, I would suggest that this regulation be changed, and that, in every case, the pauper be required to prove in what electoral division he has spent the longest continuous period out of the last (say) five years, and that he be in all cases charged against such electoral division, and so continue as long as he remains chargeable.

This plan, no doubt, does not effect all that is desirable, but stimulates to exertion in two ways. It places it within the reach of almost every proprietor to escape the able-bodied rate, by affording employment to that class; and it throws an additional burden on those who persevere in doing nothing. These, it will be admitted, are two very important points gained; and while promoting them it, in the first place, avoids all the complication and detail of account required for the townland rating, as it is only necessary that care be taken that every pauper put on the books of an electoral division should have his own townland accurately noted. This is supposed to be done at present, and by a little care can be strictly enforced.

2nd. The rate for the helpless poor, as well as the possible contingency of a rate in aid, is sufficient to keep up a community of interest, and to prevent that severance and limitation of attention to individual property, and consequent neglect of the concerns of the union, which might be the consequence of the purely townland rating.

3rd. The above, to a certain degree, also answers the third objection stated to the townland system.

4th. There is no doubt that some townlands which have been cleared, as well as farms entirely applied to grazing purposes, will, as is objected to the townland system, also under the plan now proposed, reap an undue advantage; but the rate in aid will reach such cases and so far mitigate them; besides, it is to be hoped that, practically speaking, such cases of exemption will bear but a small proportion to those where exemption will be obtained by stimulated exertion on the part of those concerned *.

5th. As to inducement to prospective clearance of exter-mination, it is to be hoped that such cases will be met by the recent Act in reference thereto. But it can readily be shown that to this proposal the objection does not apply ; but that, on the contrary, as compared with the present state of the Poor Law, it must act to discourage, and not to encourage, extermination. A proprietor now anxious to relieve his property from an over-population, has, after effecting a clearance, merely to bear his proportion of the increase caused in the rate of the electoral division for the support of the parties ejected—a very small drawback, com-pared to the great benefit arising from the local relief. But, under the system proposed, a landlord—anxious as any one would be to exempt his townlands from taxation—can, under ordinary circumstances, do so by the employment of the able-bodied resident thereon ; but, should he have driven therefrom any large number of his paupers to another estate, any one of these (who for two years and a-half are, by the present law, chargeable as against their former residences) obtaining relief, disentitled him to such exemption ; and this is a circumstance against which no vigilance or exertion on his part can protect him.

I trust that the foregoing makes out my case of miti-gating, where it does not altogether remove, the evils now complained of; while it avoids the chief parts of the objections made to the proposed system of townland rating; and I therefore, with some degree of confidence, entreat your Excellency's powerful aid to have these sugges-tions carried into effect.

---

* It might be advisable to limit exemption to cases where it is shown that a certain average of employment of labour has been afforded.

H

# APPENDIX, D.

*Extracts from the Report of* GEORGE NICHOLLS, Esq. *on Irish Poor Laws.*

*Paragraph* 115.—Emigration ought not, I think, under any circumstances, to be looked to as an ordinary resource. An excess of population is an evil: to relieve that excess by emigration is so far good; but it may be doubted whether the parent stock is not enfeebled by the remedy thus applied. In general, the most active and enterprising emigrate, leaving the more feeble and less robust and resolute at home. Thus a continual drain of its best elements lowers the tone and reduces the general vigour of the community, at the same time that it imparts an additional stimulus to the tendency towards an undue increase of population, which was the immediate cause of the disease.

*Paragraph* 116.—In saying this I do not contend against the resort to emigration as a relief from an existing evil, but merely wish to point out the inexpediency of encouraging it as an improved practice in our social system. The necessity for its adoption should be regarded as an indication of disease, which it would be better to prevent than to relieve. The means of prevention will be found in the education and improved moral and prudential habits of the community. In proportion as these prevail will its general character be elevated, and individuals will feel a wholesome dread of entailing upon themselves burthens which will depress their position in the social scale. In Ireland, unhappily, these prudential considerations do not prevail at all, or prevail in a very imperfect degree; and the consequence is, that marriages are daily contracted with the most reckless improvidence. Boys and girls marry, literally without habitation or any means of support, trusting, as they say, to Providence, as others have done before them. It is quite lamentable to witness the effects of this ignorant recklessness, which, by occasioning an excessively rapid increase in their numbers, tends to depress the whole population, and to extend the sphere of wretchedness and want."

*Paragraph* 117. — Emigration not only may, but I believe must, be had recourse to, as a present means of relief, whenever the population becomes excessive in any district and no opening for migration can be found. The actual excess of population will be indicated by the pressure of able-bodied labourers upon the workhouse. If any considerable number of these enter the workhouse and remain there subject to its discipline, it may be taken as a proof of their actual inability to provide for themselves, and of the consequent excess of labourers beyond the means of employment. Under such circumstances emigration must be looked to as the best, if not the only present remedy ; and express provision should, I think, be made in the Act for defraying the expense which this would occasion, as well as for the regulations under which it should be carried into effect.

*Paragraph* 118.—With reference to the expense I propose that the charge of emigration should in every case be equally born by the Government and the union from which the emigrants proceed. This division of the charge appears to me to be equitable ; for although the union only is immediately benefited, yet eventually the whole empire is relieved, excess in one portion of it tending to occasion an excess in the whole. The emigration should, I think, be limited to a British colony, where such arrangements might be made, through the intervention of the Colonial Office, as would serve to protect the emigrants on their first arrival and also ensure their obtaining employment at the earliest period. This is important alike for themselves and the community : at home they were a burthen; in their new position they will increase the general productive powers of the empire, as well as enlarge the demand for British pro-duce. In every case, however, the emigration should be conducted under the control of the central authority, and be subjected to such regulations as the Government may deem it right to establish.

## APPENDIX, E.

*Facts relative to the present Condition of Unions in the West and South of Ireland.*

THE daily newspapers and other periodical publications have for some time past abounded with statements relative to the condition of the poor and the working of the Poor Law in every part of Ireland. Some of these statements are doubtless entitled to full confidence, but in many instances they appear to be more or less influenced by the particular opinions or interests of the writer. I have thought that it might be useful that a person accustomed to inquiries of this nature, and beyond the reach of local influences, should endeavour to ascertain the real condition of some of the poorer districts. For this purpose I have visited several parts of the West and South of Ireland, and have besides sought for accurate information from persons upon whom I was able to place reliance. I have been disappointed in my hopes of collecting a mass of statistical information, which appeared proper to throw light upon the subjects discussed in the text, but I believe that the following statements may be relied upon as possessing as much accuracy as the nature of the subject admits :—

### Ballina, Castlebar, Clifden, and Westport Unions.

The four above-named unions, comprising the extreme west of Connaught, so far resemble each other in the general circumstances of their condition that, to avoid repetition, I shall speak of them together. I should premise that my personal inquiries have been confined to Westport union; but I have been furnished with information respecting the other unions above named from the most trustworthy sources. A general idea of the condition and resources of these unions may be formed from the following table:—

| Union. | Area of statute acres. | Population in 1841. | Poor Law valuation. | No. of acres under crops in 1847. | Proportion of rated value to population. |
|---|---|---|---|---|---|
| | | | £. | | £. s. d. |
| Ballina . | 504,115 | 120,787 | 95,774 | 38,038 | 15 10 |
| Castlebar . | 160,687 | 61,063 | 50,981 | 20,421 | 16 8 |
| Clifden . | 189,504 | 33,465 | 22,426 | 5,527 | 13 5 |
| Westport . | 330,176 | 77,952 | 38,876 | 16,168 | 10 0 |
| Total | 1,184,482 | 293,267 | 208,057 | 80,154 | 14 2 |

We have here an area greater than that of the county of Northumberland, with a population one-sixth more numerous, while the annual value of rateable property is to that in Northumberland as 2 to 13, or, more properly speaking, this was the proportion before the failure of the potato crops reduced more than half of the population to pauperism, and at the same time diminished in nearly the same ratio the actual sources from which the support of the poor is to be derived. The district, including these and some portions of the adjoining unions, presents the widest example of the disastrous effects of the cottier tenure of land amongst a population accustomed to a low standard of comfort, and unused to regular industry or economy. Large properties were granted by the chief proprietors, in long leases, at low money rents. Upon these the process of continual sub-division was carried on without interference from the land-lord, usually too neglectful to heed the practice, but unable effectually to check it, even when desirous of so doing, owing to the expensive and uncertain operation of the law. A population subsisting altogether upon potatoes continued to increase even beyond the limit at which they could assure themselves a regular supply of that food. Holdings were continually subdivided, squatters settled upon the most barren spots, and a large proportion of the inhabitants were accustomed to eke out the deficient supply of potatoes during the summer season by sea-weed, limpets, and such garbage as they could collect upon the sea-coast, whither in conse-quence the great affluence of population naturally directed itself.

Less even than elsewhere in Ireland was there any trace of the class of regular agricultural labourers. The larger farmers employed their land in grazing cattle or in sheep pasture; and their demand for labour was almost limited to one or two servant boys, employed as herds or to assist in the tillage of a few acres. The concurrent effect of the famine and the extension of the Poor Law has been to cause a large portion of the smaller holders to give up their land; thousands of acres have been surrendered to proprietors and middlemen; but the constant drain of capital in a district, always wretchedly poor, has made it equally impossible for these parties to cultivate the land themselves, or to find tenants capable of so doing. The fisheries, though con-ducted with insufficient capital, and deficient energy and skill, largely contributed to the support of the population in times past; but in the present utterly impoverished con-dition of the country they have completely failed, except where supported in two places by the establishment of curing-stations, one of which has, I am informed, been abandoned.

To complete the parallel between the unions here mentioned and the county of Northumberland, we should remark that four unions here contain 41 electoral divisions, with an average of 28,890 acres and 7152 inhabitants to each division, while in Northumberland 12 unions contain 537 parishes, with an average of 2189 acres and 495 inhabitants to each parish. If abuses of various kinds exist in these western unions, if improper persons are admitted to relief, if relieving officers defraud the poor or the ratepayers, if there is a total absence of general co-operation for the administration of the law, it must be admitted that this is no more than might be expected where the interests and local knowledge of individuals are utterly lost in districts of such unmanageable extent.

Public attention has recently been directed to the fact that in spite of the pressure of pauperism in these unions, the rates imposed have not borne any adequate proportion to the rated value; the poundage-rates struck for the year ending September 29, 1848, being an average of four shillings in Ballina and Westport unions, and five shillings in Castlebar union, while those struck in October 1848 have varied from three to five shillings. These rates have been made, not upon an estimate of the sum really required for the support of the destitute poor, but solely with a view to the means of the ratepayers. The following table shows the rate of expenditure for the week ending January 6, 1849:—

| UNION. | Number relieved in Workhouse. | Number on out-door Relief. | Cost of Workhouse Relief. | | Cost of out-door Relief. | | Estimated Cost of Establishment. | Total weekly Cost. | |
|---|---|---|---|---|---|---|---|---|---|
| | | | £. | s. | £. | s. | £. | £. | s. |
| Ballina . . | 2679 | 16,849 | 181 | 16 | 534 | 10 | 180 | 896 | 6 |
| Castlebar . . | 1561 | 8,309 | 118 | 14 | 214 | 2 | 85 | 417 | 16 |
| Westport . . | 1528 | 9,250 | 114 | 11 | 174 | 2 | 80 | 368 | 13 |

But it is important to observe that these sums do not represent the real cost of giving an adequate subsistence to the destitute poor. In Westport union the weekly expenditure for each individual receiving out-door relief is not more than fourpence halfpenny. Owing to the embarrassed state of the finances, and the difficulty of obtaining any supplies whatever from the contractors, the allowance of one pound of meal per day to each adult and half that quantity for children, which is usually deemed the minimum of human subsistence, is reduced by one-fourth or one-third, and the unfortunate paupers are merely kept alive in an enfeebled and emaciated condition.

Again, to judge from the past year, we must expect the demands for out-door relief to increase very much as the season advances, and we should fix the average expenditure for the entire year above the point which it has attained in January.

Omitting, however, to take either of these circumstances into account, and neglecting moreover the actual liabilities of these unions, though considerable (amounting in Westport union to more than £.6000), we shall have the following estimate of the annual cost of relief:—

|  | | | | £. | s. | d. |
|---|---|---|---|---|---|---|
| Ballina | . | . | . | 46,607 | 12 | 0 |
| Castlebar | . | . | . | 21,725 | 12 | 0 |
| Westport | . | . | . | 19,169 | 16 | 0 |

But these sums not being assessed uniformly, we should require poundage-rates, varying from seven to fifteen shillings, on the several electoral divisions. It might be just possible to collect the first-named rate in some of the less impoverished divisions, but those in which a fifteen-shilling rate would be required are precisely the districts so utterly pauperised that it is almost impossible to levy the current rates of three or four shillings. Instances are now frequent of seizures for poor-rate in which the only property

found by the collector is household furniture and bedding*,
so that the operation of the law is to create directly, and by
no circuitous process, the very destitution which it attempts
to relieve.   Upon minute inquiry I find that the most
extensive proprietor in Westport union has received during
the year 1848 from the tenant-farmers upon his estate very
little more than the amount of poor-rate for which he was
liable as immediate lessor of holdings rated below £.4,
added to the tithe rent-charge and the cost of collection.
This state of things, in which the surplus income of a district,
over and above the actual subsistence of the cultivators of
the soil, is so small in proportion to the sum necessary for
the support of the destitute poor, exhibits an instance of the
condition of society in which the working of a Poor Law
becomes in reality an impossibility.   I confess that the
result of observation has satisfied me that the limit assigned
in the text, by which five shillings in the pound should be
required from the electoral division, and two shillings and
sixpence from the union, before assistance should be given
for emigration, is too high for the poorer unions in the West
of Ireland.   The reason of this is that the valuation of land
under a system of potato culture is no longer applicable at
the present time.   In order to make the proposed limit
practically serviceable in a few of the poorer unions it would
be necessary to fix the limit at about two-thirds of that
which I have proposed as the general rule.

The diminution of the population has been one of the
most apparent results of the successive failures of the potato
crop in these unions.   Three causes have produced this
result :—The frightful mortality of the winter 1846-1847;
the emigration, or migration to other districts, of the
smaller holders of land, who have either voluntarily given
up their holdings or been evicted by their landlords; lastly,

---

* The seizure of bedding for poor-rate, though a frequent practice, is
of doubtful legality.

the diminished number of births by which the ordinary equilibrium of the population is maintained. It is not possible to arrive at accurate results for a large district, but I believe that the following return for the electoral division of Ballyhean, in Castlebar union, may be relied upon:—

| BALLINA UNION. | | | | CASTLEBAR UNION. | | |
|---|---|---|---|---|---|---|
| Ballysokeery Electoral Division, Population in 1841, 6034. | | | | Ballyhean Electoral Division, Population in 1841, 4032. | | |
| Year. | Births. | Marriages. | Deaths. | Births. | Marriages. | Deaths. |
| 1845 | — | — | — | 136 | 22 | 25* |
| 1846 | 25 | 4 | 300 | 127 | 17 | 110 |
| 1847 | 19 | 3 | 355 | 54 | 6 | 258 |
| 1848 | 26 | 4 | 200 | 28 | 3 | 178 |

Showing a diminution from increased mortality and diminished births of 354, or nearly nine per cent. on the population, within three years. I am compelled, however, to believe that the mortality was very much greater in some districts.

Allowing 12 per cent. for the increase of population from 1841 to 1846, and borrowing from a subsequent return the number of emigrants who have left these electoral divisions during the last two years, we have the following general results:—

| Electoral Division. | Probable Population in January 1846. | Excess of Deaths over Births during the last 3 years. | Number of Emigrants during the last 2 years. | Loss of Population during the last 3 years. | Per Centage of diminution in Population. |
|---|---|---|---|---|---|
| Ballysokeery. | 6758 | 785 | 1114 | 1899 | 28 |
| Ballyhean .. | 4516 | 337 | 184 | 521 | 11½ |

The probable population of Westport union in 1846 was about 87,000, and allowing 20,000 excess of deaths over births and 5000 to have gone away, there would remain 62,000. Marriages have diminished to about one-

* Apparently a mistake, or error in copying.

sixth of the former number, and births have fallen off to nearly an equal extent. Emigration and migration to England and Scotland have proceeded most extensively in Ballina, and to a considerable extent in the other unions. I have obtained from trustworthy sources the following returns from two electoral divisions in Ballina and Castlebar unions respectively:—

| Union. | Electoral Division. | Number of Families who have Emigrated or Migrated | Number of Individuals composing those Families. | Number of Families who were holders of land. | Total number of acres occupied by them. | Number of Families occupying land who departed without paying rent. | Number of Families who are known to have emigrated to N. America. | Number of Families in Great Britain, or destination not known. | Total area of Electoral Division in statute acres. | Population of Electoral Division in 1841. |
|---|---|---|---|---|---|---|---|---|---|---|
| Ballina | Ballysokeery | 234 | 1114 | 234 | 1459 | 193 | 153 | 81 | 12,692 | 6034 |
| Castlebar | Ballyhean | 81 | 184 | 36 | 148 | 27 | 56 | 25 | 7,731 | 4032 |

It may appear almost paradoxical to assert that at a time when so great a diminution of the population has been effected, without any direct interference to promote emigration, a further decrease should be required. To understand the peculiar grounds on which this conclusion depends, it is necessary to consider that this part of Ireland has maintained a population occupying the mere margin of civilisation, producing sufficient means of subsistence for themselves, but a very small surplus from which capital could accumulate. Upon the occurrence of the calamity which has reduced the largest portion of them to destitution, no resources are found from which the necessities of the destitute can be adequately supplied.

One of the most disastrous consequences of the change which has reduced a great part of the population to idleness and dependence on public support, is the utter insecurity of property in these districts. Robberies and thefts of all kinds have increased to a most serious extent, and offer a formidable check to the efforts of improving farmers, or the introduction of new capital into these unfortunate districts.

A letter from Mr. Graham, a proprietor in Clifden union, published some weeks ago in the " Times," contains so clear a statement of the condition of western proprietors that I am induced to reprint it :—

TO THE EDITOR OF THE TIMES.

*Ballinakill, Clifden, County of Galway, December* 1, 1848.

Sir,—Being convinced that it is the wish of your journal to be set right on every point connected with the present crisis in Ireland, I beg to say, in the leading article of the " Times," dated 17th November, it is stated, that no landlord can for a moment hesitate about the expediency of embarking a large sum in giving employment, and thereby relieving the destitution, in place of allowing the paupers on his estate to remain in half-starved idleness, as recipients of out-door relief; and, "if his private resources do not enable " him to adopt this course, by a recent enactment of the " Legislature, he can procure money from Government as " a loan for the purpose." You are evidently not aware that by the present Poor Law, the hands of every landlord and ratepayer, anxious to discharge the duties of property in this, and, I may say, in every other respect, are completely paralysed, as they are not only liable to pay an equal portion towards the support of the destitution existing on the badly-managed properties of their neighbours, but also, by an extraordinary perversion of every principle of justice and common sense, the more employment they give the larger amount of rate they will have to pay, though, probably, most of those individuals to whom that employment has been afforded belong to and reside on other estates, as, when capital is expended on the improvement or reclamation of waste land, a revision takes place, and the rated value is increased to an enormous degree, though the improvement effected is not, nor will be for some time, reproductive. A few facts will exemplify this fully. I am a proprietor in the Clifden union, in which there were at one period last summer 21,000 persons receiving relief, out of a population of 30,000. The properties in it are principally of large acreable extent, and nearly one-half the landlords are most anxious that the poor of each estate should be supported by employment given on it by themselves and their tenants, and would guarantee this being effectually done ; but owing to the present state of the law, and the great destitution existing, it is impossible to carry it out, without having also to pay a larger proportion of rate (on account of the improvements which would be made) to support the poor of non-resident and unimproving landlords in other parts of this extensive union, forty miles long, than would fall to the lot of those very proprietors themselves to pay. A Lancashire gentleman, son to Mr. Eastwood, of Brindle Lodge, near Preston, who has got a lease for ever from me of a large improveable tract, and who in the two years he has resided here, has expended between £.4000 and £.5000 on it, having employed on the average fifty labourers daily, and in summer sometimes as many as 120, most of them belonging to the properties of other proprietors, and there not being one single pauper on the large townland on which he resides, containing 2658 acres, on the valuation of the union being revised the other day, had his improvements valued at an increase of £.115 a year, though none of them are as yet in the slightest degree reproductive. The result is Mr. Eastwood has dismissed all his labourers, except twelve ; and until a change in the law takes place, has completely ceased all his improvements and employment, by which so many families were supported, who are now thrown on the union as recipients of out-door relief. Another gentleman, Mr. Prior, who has a similar lease from me, and obtained from Government

£.800 as a loan, under the Act you refer to in your article of the 17th ult., the first instalment of which, £.160, he has already laid out on his farm, having previously expended a large amount of private capital on it, had his improvements, effected with this Government money, valued, and his rates increased in an equal manner; the consequence of which is, that he wrote last week to the Government, saying he must decline taking the remainder of the £.800, as his doing so would make him liable to pay a greater sum than he even now does, to support the paupers of other estates. A third gentleman, Mr. Crauford Butler, of the county of Carlow, who has also a lease for ever on this estate, and has likewise obtained a loan of £.1000 from Government, with two instalments of which, £.400, he has made great improvements, and has reclaimed a good deal of waste ground, having with it, latterly, and with his own private resources for years previously, given most general and extensive employment—having at one period above two hundred men at work daily—has, from the same cause, expressed his determination not to take the remainder of his loan, and has reduced largely the number of his labourers. I mention these facts to show that the attempt has been literally made to carry out your suggestions here, as well as many other parts of Ireland; but owing to the principles of the present Poor Law, the boon granted by the Legislature to benefit the country, by facilitating improvement and employment, is completely nullified; and until the law with respect to improvements on land, being subject to increased rate for a certain extended period, is altered, and until each property or townland is directly liable to support the destitution existing on it, by employment or otherwise, the hands of every man, whether improving landlord or industrious farmer, are completely tied, and the position of this country must go from bad to worse, the laying out of capital on land being completely put a stop to. A Poor Law is essentially necessary, but it should not be so constituted as effectually to swamp individual exertion, and confound, in one chaos, the good and the bad—those who are desirous of discharging the duties property involves, and those who are not. The many other evils connected with the present system of Poor Laws, and its ruinous consequences to the most vital interests of every class of the community, from the landlord, whose property is confiscated, and the farmer, the fruits of whose industry are swept away by it, down to the pauper who is utterly demoralised by its gratuitous and enervating bounty, I leave to those who will bring them forward more forcibly than I can; but I trust you will use the information I have given you for the purpose of removing the very erroneous impression of the apathy of Irish landlords, which your article of the 17th ult. must have given rise to, and of laying the position in which this country is placed fairly before the British public.

I have the honour to be, Sir,
Your most faithful Servant,

FRANCIS J. GRAHAM.

---

## DUNGARVAN, KANTURK, and LISTOWEL UNIONS.

The condition of Munster differs in some essential respects from that of the west of Connaught. I have been able to collect some information with reference to three unions in different parts of the province, which represent pretty fairly the condition of the counties in which they are respectively situated.

### DUNGARVAN UNION.

This union comprises the central part of the county of Waterford, with an area of 151,832 statute acres, valued for Poor Law rating at £.94,591, and having a population of

68,642 inhabitants, according to the census of 1841. I have been able to obtain but little accurate information with respect to this union, which is the more to be regretted as it exhibits in a remarkable degree the most striking contrasts between adjacent properties, in respect to the condition of the population and the progress of improvement.

I am acquainted with the condition of one property upon which the proprietor had been accustomed, for many years, to expend a considerable portion of his income in improvements. Barren mountain-land had been successfully reclaimed, new houses had been built for the farmers and labourers, and a considerable population subsisted in comparative prosperity. Although there is not a single pauper upon the entire estate, the proprietor paid £.600 for poor-rates during the past year, and is now liable for an equal amount for the current rate. The result has been to cause a reduction in the amount of employment given by this gentleman, and nearly the entire sum payable for the pauperism of neighbouring neglected properties, will, in effect, be deducted from the wages of labourers on his own property.

I have received some trustworthy information with reference to the amount of emigration in the western parts of this union.

The electoral division of Aglish contained 5174 inhabitants in 1841. During the years 1847 and 1848, 182 individuals emigrated, many of them single men, who it is believed will send for their families as soon as they are established in America. Of this number thirteen were farmers, occupying about 240 statute acres. The united parishes of Aglish and Whitechurch contained in 1841 a population of 8577 souls. The following return shows the comparative diminution in births and marriages :—

| | Births. | Marriages. |
|---|---|---|
| Average of four years, ending 1st November, 1846 .. | 264 | 52½ |
| Year ending 1st November, 1848 | 112 | 24 |

In the absence of an accurate registry it is impossible to ascertain with certainty the number of deaths occurring in a given time, but I am assured, upon good authority, that they amounted to not less than 1000 within the last two years, out of a population of about 9000.

## KANTURK UNION.

This union has an area of 256,892 statute acres, its valuation for poor-rate is £.106,114, and its population in 1841 was 85,861. This shows about £.1 4s. 9d. of rateable value to each inhabitant; the general proportion in the province of Munster being about £.1 11s. There are about 55,000 acres in the union under crops, the remainder being for the most part mountainous pasture or bog. The following table shows the amount of rates struck and levied in the union during the year 1848, together with the proportion of rateable value to population, and the extent of cultivated land in each electoral division:—

| Electoral Division. | Poundage Rate struck in March 1848. | | Poundage Rate struck in Nov. 1848. | | Total of Rates struck in 1848. | | Population in 1841. | Proportion of Rated Value to Population | | | Acres under Crops in 1847. | Total Area in Statute Acres. |
|---|---|---|---|---|---|---|---|---|---|---|---|---|
| | s. | d. | s. | d. | s. | d. | | £. | s. | d. | | |
| Kanturk .... | 5 | 0 | 2 | 6 | 7 | 6 | 7,497 | 1 | 7 | 8 | 3649 | 14,421 |
| Castlemagner | 2 | 0 | 2 | 10 | 4 | 10 | 3,007 | 2 | 0 | 8 | 2922 | 7,842 |
| Clonmeen .. | 4 | 6 | 2 | 6 | 7 | 0 | 7,052 | 0 | 18 | 11 | 5223 | 21,845 |
| Cullen...... | 5 | 0 | 2 | 6 | 7 | 6 | 5,490 | 1 | 1 | 11 | 3103 | 13,675 |
| Drishane .. | 3 | 0 | 2 | 4 | 5 | 4 | 8,868 | 1 | 1 | 7 | 4295 | 29,885 |
| Droumtariff . | 6 | 0 | 2 | 6 | 8 | 6 | 7,271 | 1 | 1 | 5 | 4255 | 15,235 |
| Kilbolane .. | 4 | 6 | 2 | 6 | 7 | 0 | 4,155 | 1 | 11 | 2 | 2848 | 9,884 |
| Kilbrin .... | 4 | 6 | 2 | 4 | 6 | 10 | 6,926 | 1 | 9 | 1 | 5088 | 14,169 |
| Kilmeen .... | 5 | 0 | 3 | 0 | 8 | 0 | 10,380 | 0 | 17 | 1 | 6044 | 36,708 |
| Knocktemple. | 5 | 0 | 2 | 6 | 7 | 6 | 2,933 | 1 | 3 | 0 | 2800 | 5,696 |
| Newmarket.. | 3 | 6 | 1 | 6 | 5 | 0 | 8,863 | 1 | 3 | 9 | 5601 | 45,778 |
| Nohavaldaly . | 2 | 6 | 2 | 6 | 5 | 0 | 3,954 | 1 | 1 | 1 | 2340 | 16,371 |
| Shandrum .. | 2 | 6 | 2 | 2 | 4 | 8 | 6,187 | 1 | 18 | 10 | 4953 | 12,016 |
| Tullylease .. | 6 | 0 | 3 | 0 | 9 | 0 | 3,278 | 0 | 18 | 8 | 1746 | 8,290 |

It is seen in the above table that in the year 1848, the poundage-rates in this union have varied from 4s. 8d. to 9s.

in the pound. The total amount of rates struck for that year is £.34,828, or rather more than 32 per cent. upon the net annual value of the entire union. Owing to reductions in rent, it is probable that the entire of this taxation has been borne by the proprietors, and to this cause we may attribute the circumstance that a comparatively small number of farmers have given up their holdings for the purpose of emigrating. Those who have departed belong to the better class of small farmers. I was able to ascertain with some certainty that four persons who have gone from one property in the union had taken about £.280 in money in addition to their outfit. The result of conversations with some of the proprietors and several intelligent farmers in the union was to satisfy me that the immediate effect of the distress of the last three years, and the concurrent increase of taxation, has been to lead all classes of farmers to reduce considerably the amount of employment given to agricultural labourers. A few active proprietors have applied for loans under the Land Improvement Act, but a much larger number are deterred from so doing by the apprehension of being unable to meet the instalments of repayment required by that Act.

It will illustrate the preceding statement to give the following particulars with reference to a single property.

The estate of Curraghs, in the electoral division of Kilbrin, contains about 2300 statute acres. It is divided into 42 holdings, one of which has been sublet by a tenant to cottier subtenants. Besides the families of the tenants there are about 60 families of labourers, containing about 70 able-bodied men living upon the estate. All these labourers were formerly in constant employment with the farmers, and were allowed sixpence a-day besides their own diet. No money, however, actually passed, as the labourers invariably were allowed con-acre potato land, paid for by their wages, without which, in fact, their families could not have subsisted at that nominal rate of wages. On the failure of the potato-crop in the autumn of 1846, the farmers being seized with the panic which then prevailed, discharged all their labourers, who accordingly sought employment upon the public works. The proprietor applied for advances for drainage under Labouchere's Letter, and received £.700 in the spring of 1847; he has since received £.1700 under the Land Improvement Act; and partly with these sums, and partly from his own funds, he has kept in constant employment nearly all the labourers on the estate, and at times an additional number from the neighbourhood. The farmers have shown no disposition to take the labourers back to their employment, and at the present time not more than 10 or 12 are so employed. The proprietor now employs 57 men, but he states that on the completion of the drainage works he cannot continue to give them profitable employment. Some of the most intelligent farmers admitted that the cultivation of the land was much injured by the want of sufficient hands being employed, portion of it being imperfectly tilled, and a portion being let to run to grass; but they state that having to support 800 or 900 paupers, they cannot afford to lay out anything more upon labour. Two of these farmers said that they thought that if the property formed an electoral division to itself, the labourers would all be taken back again into employment by the farmers on the estate. A third farmer wished that all the labourers of the union should be *fairly divided* amongst the occupiers of land, but he failed to explain how they should in that case be made to work.

The gentleman above referred to is likewise a proprietor in Cullen and Droumtariff electoral divisions. In the year 1847, he attempted to induce the other proprietors in those districts to unite for the purpose of providing employment for the able-bodied poor; in the first-named division he did not receive a single answer to his letters, and, therefore, abandoned the attempt; in Droumtariff, some partial co-operation was effected, and about £.1000 was expended in drainage and improvement.

## LISTOWEL UNION.

This union, which includes the northern part of Kerry, has an area of 208,964 acres, the Poor Law valuation is £.97,558, and the population in 1841 was 78,756. These numbers show upon the average of the union a proportion of £.1 4s. 9d. rateable value to each inhabitant, which is the same that exists in Kanturk union, and is somewhat above the average for the county of Kerry. The following table shows the amount of rates struck in the union during the year 1848, together with other particulars respecting the several electoral divisions:—

| ELECTORAL DIVISION. | Poundage Rate struck in June 1848. | | Poundage Rate struck in November 1848. | | Total of Rates struck in 1848. | | Population in 1841. | Proportion of Rated Value to Population. | | | No. of Acres under Crops in 1847. | Total Area in Statute Acres. |
|---|---|---|---|---|---|---|---|---|---|---|---|---|
| | s. | d. | s. | d. | s. | d. | | £. | s. | d. | | |
| Abbeydorney . | 2 | 5 | 2 | 7 | 5 | 0 | 3142 | 1 | 8 | 0 | 1908 | 7,228 |
| Ardfert . | 3 | 0 | 6 | 6 | 9 | 6 | 3583 | 1 | 0 | 6 | 1891 | 5,633 |
| Ballyheigue . | 3 | 0 | 4 | 0 | 7 | 0 | 4795 | 0 | 14 | 5 | 1925 | 11,378 |
| Ballylongford | 3 | 0 | 5 | 10 | 8 | 10 | 6606 | 1 | 0 | 5 | 3121 | 16,761 |
| Dromkeen . | 3 | 0 | 6 | 8 | 9 | 8 | 6480 | 0 | 16 | 7 | 2950 | 11,084 |
| Duagh . . | 3 | 0 | 3 | 6 | 6 | 6 | 4411 | 1 | 3 | 5 | 3448 | 16,763 |
| Gunsborough . | 0 | 9 | 3 | 0 | 3 | 9 | 3247 | 1 | 17 | 0 | 2152 | 13,770 |
| Kilconly . | 3 | 0 | 2 | 9 | 5 | 9 | 2210 | 1 | 4 | 5 | 831 | 5,743 |
| Kilfeighny . | 3 | 0 | 3 | 2 | 6 | 2 | 2317 | 1 | 8 | 9 | 1274 | 10,232 |
| Kilflyn . | 2 | 6 | 4 | 0 | 6 | 6 | 1088 | 1 | 12 | 1 | 1012 | 6,696 |
| Killahan . | 2 | 2 | 1 | 9 | 3 | 11 | 1555 | 1 | 10 | 9 | 1078 | 4,054 |
| Killahinny . | 3 | 0 | 6 | 8 | 9 | 8 | 3050 | 0 | 18 | 3 | 1162 | 4,673 |
| Kilmoyly . | 2 | 6 | 3 | 0 | 5 | 6 | 5371 | 1 | 3 | 5 | 3790 | 9,391 |
| Kilshenane . | 3 | 0 | 4 | 3 | 7 | 3 | 2342 | 1 | 7 | 0 | 2685 | 14,655 |
| Kiltomy . | 2 | 6 | 3 | 0 | 5 | 6 | 4145 | 1 | 10 | 9 | 2220 | 12,773 |
| Knockanure . | 0 | 6 | 3 | 0 | 3 | 6 | 2012 | 1 | 18 | 0 | 989 | 8,937 |
| Lisselton . | 3 | 0 | 3 | 6 | 6 | 6 | 2638 | 1 | 5 | 10 | 1422 | 8,290 |
| Listowel . | 2 | 8 | 3 | 4 | 6 | 0 | 7715 | 1 | 9 | 1 | 3556 | 13,968 |
| Newton Sandes | 2 | 6 | 2 | 1 | 4 | 7 | 3293 | 1 | 9 | 0 | 3201 | 10,699 |
| Battoo . . | 3 | 0 | 3 | 0 | 6 | 0 | 3654 | 1 | 5 | 2 | 1972 | 7,032 |
| Tarbert . . | 0 | 9 | 3 | 0 | 3 | 9 | 5102 | 1 | 3 | 11 | 2788 | 9,204 |

The rates vary from 3*s*. 6*d*. to 9*s*. 8*d*. in the several electoral divisions. The small number in which the taxation has not exceeded a poundage-rate of 5*s*. do not appear to have suffered very much, but in the greater number of the electoral divisions of this union the symptoms of over-taxation are only too manifest. A considerable number of the middling class of farmers have emigrated during the last two years, and the practice of departing surreptitiously (usually by night) carrying away moveables, and leaving rent and other debts unpaid, has become exceedingly common. I have not yet obtained returns which would show the nature and extent of the emigration which has taken place, but from my inquiries I am persuaded that the effect as hitherto conducted has been still further to depress the condition of the labouring class, by diminishing the proportion of capital to labour. Some facts illustrative of the working of the law in this union are stated in Mr. Crosbie's letter (Appendix, C.)

1 shall close these observations by remarking that it is more especially in districts similarly circumstanced to this union, that the emigration of that portion of the labouring class who cannot be employed with the amount of capital now applied to agriculture, would contribute powerfully to the progress of improvement. A certain impulse has been given, some enterprise and capital are forthcoming, but at present they have to struggle with the depressing effects of excessive taxation; and it is to be feared, that if this should continue, enterprise will be deadened and capital unproductively wasted.

THE END.

LONDON:
PRINTED BY T. BRETTELL, RUPERT STREET, HAYMARKET.

Printed in the United States
By Bookmasters